Get the eBook FREE!

(PDF, ePub, Kindle, and liveBook all included)

We believe that once you buy a book from us, you should be able to read it in any format we have available. To get electronic versions of this book at no additional cost to you, purchase and then register this book at the Manning website.

Go to https://www.manning.com/freebook and follow the instructions to complete your pBook registration.

That's it!
Thanks from Manning!

In Praise of *Data for All*...

John Thompson's book, Data for All, *is one of the more interesting ones I have read recently. It is one of the most honest, direct, pull-no-punches sources on one of the most important personal issues of our time. That issue is, 'Should I undertake extraordinary efforts to prevent companies—tech and otherwise—from getting access to my personal data?' I think the answer is yes. I've already changed some of my own behaviors after reading the book, and I suggest you do so as well. You have more to lose than you may think.*

—Thomas H. Davenport,
Distinguished Professor, Babson College and Fellow,
MIT Initiative on the Digital Economy,
author of *Competing on Analytics* and *The AI Advantage*

John provides a cogent and concise treatment of the problem of 'digital exhaust' and what to do about the nearly infinite traces of ourselves that we create in the course of everyday activity. His voice is of someone who has lived with and thought about data from before it was trendy to do so. While John is appropriately blunt about the challenges ordinary people face in controlling their data, he is neither cynical or pessimistic, and therefore provides an actionable path toward greater agency around the data we generate.

—Thomas A. Finholt,
Dean, School of Information,
University of Michigan

How much time do you spend thinking deeply about the data you create, who is using that data, and how? It's hard to know where to even start. John Thompson's Data for All *provides a wide-ranging non-technical overview of the past, present, and future of data, of topics including data privacy, open data, and data analytics. And for those looking to take control of their own data futures, this book is the best version of a 'People's Data Manifesto' I've seen to date.*

—David Steier,
Distinguished Service Professor,
Carnegie Mellon University

John Thompson and I have been discussing, debating, and collaborating on data and analytics projects for over 25 years. Data for All *concisely summarizes and accurately outlines the coming data revolution and, at the same time, provides guidance as to how each individual and company can prepare themselves to own, manage, protect, and profit from their data. The world of data is changing rapidly. All of us should be ready to benefit from it, and this book is a practical guide to doing just that.*

—Larry Smarr,
Distinguished Prof. Emeritus,
UC San Diego Department of Computer Science & Engineering

Data for All

JOHN K. THOMPSON

FOREWORD BY THOMAS H. DAVENPORT

MANNING

SHELTER ISLAND

For online information and ordering of this and other Manning books, please visit
www.manning.com. The publisher offers discounts on this book when ordered in quantity.
For more information, please contact

Special Sales Department
Manning Publications Co.
20 Baldwin Road
PO Box 761
Shelter Island, NY 11964
Email: orders@manning.com

Manning Publications Co.   Development editor: Ian Hough
20 Baldwin Road   Technical editor: Gabor Gollnhofer
PO Box 761   Review editor: Adriana Sabo
Shelter Island, NY 11964   Production editor: Andy Marinkovich
                                            Proofreader: Jason Everett
                                             Typesetter: Gordan Salinovic
                                         Cover designer: Marija Tudor

ISBN 9781633438774
Printed in the United States of America

brief contents

contents

Appendices 1-5 are available in the eBook only. Read online in liveBook.

foreword

John Thompson's book, *Data for All*, for which I am pleased to write a few words of introduction, is one of the more interesting ones I have read recently. I am not yet entirely sure that I agree with everything he writes—there are some pretty strong statements about individuals and companies in here—but I am very glad I read it. It is one of the most honest, direct, pull-no-punches sources on one of the most important personal issues of our time. That issue is, "Should I undertake extraordinary efforts to prevent companies—tech and otherwise—from getting access to my personal data?"

I think the answer is yes, but my own thinking has evolved somewhat on this issue. I love John's personal and historical stories in this book, so I will provide one too. In 1998 I saw the movie *Enemy of the State* with Will Smith in the starring role and an excellent cast overall. I highly recommend seeing the movie, even if you are not interested in data privacy. But if you are, it raises a particularly interesting set of issues. Will Smith plays a lawyer named Bobby Dean. He accidentally ends up with some highly damaging information about a government intelligence agency. A corrupt member of that agency is able to use all of the data about Dean to track him down instantaneously, tap into all his calls, plant all sorts of false information about him, and generally make his life miserable.

In 1998 that wasn't really possible; data couldn't be captured, integrated, and acted upon instantaneously. Today, however, the Will Smith character would have left a much richer data trail, and the communications and computing power available to the intelligence agency would make it relatively easy to track and find him (and perhaps to shoot him dead with a drone!).

The situation is somewhat similar with today's tech companies, or just any company that wants to sell you something. Like the intelligence industry near the turn of the century, their tools aren't really that good yet. I constantly receive "targeted" and "personalized" ads that are of no interest to me at all. I am often "retargeted" with offers for goods I once searched for or stumbled upon online. The assumption isn't very sophisticated—if I was once interested, I must still be. Even if I actually bought the thing, the advertiser doesn't seem to be aware, or assumes I want two.

But like the intelligence industry, advertisers will eventually get much better at targeting their messages to consumers based on what they know about them. At some point we will undoubtedly all be shocked, embarrassed, or creeped out by the things that are known about us and acted upon by commercial organizations. As Thompson points out, tech companies—and sometimes just retailers and consumer goods companies—know who and where you are, what you've bought in the past (at their site and elsewhere), what you look at on social media, what you say to Alexa, what you email to your friends and colleagues, etc. It's clearly too much.

And the tech industry has never been sympathetic or empathetic to our privacy concerns. As then-Sun Microsystems CEO Scott McNealy famously replied in 1999 when a group of reporters asked him about data privacy, "You have zero privacy anyway. Get over it." Ten years later, Eric Schmidt, at the time the CEO of Google, said in a CNBC interview in 2009 that "If you have something that you don't want anyone to know, maybe you shouldn't be doing it in the first place." That's a pretty scary thought, given that probably everyone has a few things they wouldn't want anyone to know. Most tech executives have become a bit more savvy in what they admit about privacy, but outside of Apple, which has wisely embraced privacy as a marketing tool, no one in Silicon Valley seems to take the issue seriously.

In short, John Thompson is correct to warn you about the perils of your online data, and it's clear that—at least in the US—nobody is going to solve this problem but you. This book gives you the information and the recommendations necessary to make things better. Now very few of us will want to go off the grid entirely, and it's really hard to do anyway. Evan Ratliff, a writer for *Wired,* tried (with a big cash reward if he succeeded) to do it for a month in 1999, took many extraordinary measures, and was found in 23 days.

But as Thompson details in this book, there are many steps you can take to reduce the exposure of your data and maintain some degree of privacy. I've already changed some of my own behaviors after reading the book, and I suggest you do so as well. You have more to lose than you may think.

—THOMAS H. DAVENPORT, DISTINGUISHED PROFESSOR,
BABSON COLLEGE AND FELLOW,
MIT INITIATIVE ON THE DIGITAL ECONOMY,
AUTHOR OF *COMPETING ON ANALYTICS* AND *THE AI ADVANTAGE*

preface

Recorded data (day-tuh) has been part of the human experience for thousands of years. The first piece of recorded and validated data is from the area now known as the Democratic Republic of Congo. The 20,000-year-old Ishango Bone—found near one of the sources of the Nile—seems to use matched tally marks on the thigh bone of a baboon for recording counts. Counts of what, we are not certain, but it is clear that marks on the bone were made with a purpose and over time.

Five thousand years ago, the Sumerians took the art and science of accounting to a new level. All manner of transactions, interactions, and exchanges between people across the cities of Mesopotamia were recorded using cuneiform on small clay tablets that could be held easily in one hand. The thousands of clay tablets can be considered the first handheld devices! Those small, terra-cotta clay tablets illustrate the extent and widespread use of data to record transactions of all types.

People have traded and transacted for nearly all of human history. I am sure that there are data and records that have yet to be discovered that predate even the Ishango Bone. At this point in time, we have discovered that our ancestors were interested in knowing and recording how many vessels of wine were bought and sold, how many heads of livestock were traded, and we have learned what transactions represented exchanges executed on that day and the promises that were made in the market each day for future trades and transactions, and much more.

In addition to the basic numbers of items traded and the prices of those items, other related data was recorded on those tablets, including the conditions that would govern the proportions and amounts, which would change based on market conditions and outcomes of external factors and events. The conditions recorded are the precursors of modern trading systems—puts and calls, short and long sales, and more.

Our forbearers realized that creating a written record that all parties were present for, and agreed to, was the most effective way to ensure that the details of any and all transactions and covenants were accurately documented and certified by not only the primary parties to the transaction, but also additional interested parties and perhaps impartial third-party observers. And for at least tens of thousands of years, we have incontrovertible proof that humans have created data to support our memory of the facts of interactions, promises, terms, conditions, timing, restrictions, correspondence, transactions and more.

The Sumerian clay tablets show that current and future transactions of considerable complexity were impressed upon the soft clay and hardened for all history. Those early records that were lost to history and found centuries later are a harbinger of the durability of data. These clay tablets are a corollary to the data we create and carelessly dump onto the internet and record for posterity on the World Wide Web.

I think back to my years as a college student, and even back to some of the things that I thought and said in high school, and I am grateful that there were no easy ways to record audio or photographs of those foolish thoughts or acts. I was trying on concepts and positions. I was encouraged by teaching and challenged by adults. I tried arguments for the sake of hearing how they worked or landed.

One example of the exuberance and folly of youth was that I represented myself in traffic court at 16. I am certain that my arguments were not persuasive, or logical. Clearly, they were not successful. I am sure that there are written records of the interactions between the judge and me, and I am equally confident that I would be embarrassed to read what I said and posited, but I didn't have any experience in court, and I tried arguments that I am sure amused the judge. I know that I did not offend him, but in the end I was directed to leave the court room and pay my fines.

Think back to your youth—did you do or say things that you may have regretted soon after? Have you done things that you are grateful are not documented in pictures, video, and audio? I am sure that this is the case for many of us.

Our children are not so lucky as to be given the chance to allow youthful folly to be so easily relegated to the dustbin of history. They will have an indelible and enduring record of some truly unfortunate moments that illustrated their early attempts to try out different courses of action or possible approaches to situations, or simply their regrettable lapses of judgment. Young people should be allowed to explore thoughts and ideas without those explorations haunting them for the rest of their lives. I am not advocating for covering up misdeeds or shirking responsibility for acts that are illegal, unethical, or harmful. What I am saying is that one episode of trying out a discredited philosophy from the pages of history or a new and novel ideology should not brand a person for the remainder of their lives.

A few of my college friends were enthralled by Marx, Engels, socialism, communism, and other early twentieth century movements, governments, and social experiments.

We were taught history and we tried on these arguments and positions for the sake of learning and experimentation. Some of those late-night discussions went far down various rabbit holes. If those discussions were to come to light via video, it would take a significant amount of explaining to lay out the context of those verbal exchanges. And we would have to explain our truly unfortunate fashion choices as well, and that would likely be more embarrassing than explaining some late-night diatribe about the value of labor, or about property rights as a basis of an economic system.

The point to be made here is that data has a long life; longer than you can imagine at first glance. Even data that was created to mark the trade of a handful of livestock 20,000 years ago can be read, remembered, and analyzed today. With our ubiquitous computing networks and modern electronic infrastructure, the audio files you record, the pictures you take, and the videos you record and send can, and might, outlive generations of your descendants. It's something to keep in mind as you snap pictures, share documents, and record voicemails.

acknowledgments

It all started with Jennifer H. Thompson saying, "You should write a book." My response was, "I have no time." As with many things in life, she persisted, and now writing is a pure joy. I cannot conceive of not writing. As with all good things in life, she knows where true joy and fulfillment can be found and enjoyed. Thank you, Jennifer. You are my partner in all things in this life and maybe others as well. We have grown, smiled, cried, and laughed all along. You are the shining light of my life. Thank you for agreeing to take my phone number on the corner of Southport and Belmont on that sunny July day in Chicago. Thank you for being the love and light of my life.

Irene Ellis was my maternal grandmother. I don't know what she saw in me, and she never told me, but all I know is that she believed in me and loved me when it felt like no one else did. From my earliest memories, she was always there with a kind smile and a hug. She was gentle, interested, and interesting to me. Thank you for showing me that all you need is one person to believe in you to make it possible to believe in yourself, and for the chocolate-covered cherries.

Kathryn Thompson is a force. Creative, intelligent, empathetic, sympathetic, and deeply caring. I am amazed at the breadth of your creativity and range of interests. Our time together is always a joy, and I love to spend time talking and laughing. You have been so generous in teaching me about how the world works and how you see life. Thank you for helping me see the way the world is today.

Zachary Thompson is witty, intelligent, observant, and deeply thoughtful. I watch, listen, and learn each day from you. Your approach to life, people, relationships, work, and play is rooted in a view that enables everyone to enjoy themselves without taking away from any one person. I am constantly impressed with your ability to be open and welcoming to the actions and views of others. This is an ability I have not internalized, but you keep showing me a better way, each day. Thank you.

Joann E. Thompson is my sister. She has been there my entire life. Sometimes I didn't pay attention or understand what it meant to me for her to always be there, but she has been. Steadfast in her support of me and all that I have tried, and in some cases, royally messed up. Thank you for being there to laugh, cry, and make me smile. You are the best sister I could have ever asked for.

about this book

This book is intended for all people who are interested in, and possibly concerned about, the data that they are continuously and consistently creating as a by-product of their online actions and almost all activities of their everyday life, and the data that commercial companies, governments, academic institutions, non-governmental agencies, not-for-profits, market research firms, data syndication companies, and other interested parties are collecting and creating about you, your children, your spouse, your parents, and everyone that you know . . . and everyone that you do not know as well.

Daily life has changed dramatically in the past hundred years. When I was a child, I grew up in a rural area dominated by farming and small manufacturing. A person could have grown up, lived, and died without creating a single piece of electronic data; the majority of people did. Computers were primarily in military and academic institutions, and the internet, or even the concept of a computer network, had not been conceived.

Sixty years ago, data was not something anyone thought about, because the amount of data we created over our lifetimes was minuscule, disconnected, hard to create, and nearly impossible to access, manage, change, or use for any purposes beyond the specific purpose that the data was created for.

I am talking about *all* data that we created about ourselves as individuals, and all the data that the companies and entities that we interacted with created about us. In 1960, you could fit all the data about an adult in the US in a small notebook. If you were interested in the electronic data about an adult in the US at that same date in time, if you printed it, that data would easily fit on one 8x11 sheet of paper. The electronic data probably consisted of your name, date of birth, and Social Security Number (national identifier). That is it.

For those readers who were not with us in 1960, an example may help clarify data in this bygone era. My father took me to the local bank branch to open an account when I was 8 years old. No appointment needed, we walked in, and we were greeted by Jim. Jim was the bank manager. We went to Jim's office. Jim, not a teller, pulled out a form from a drawer behind his desk and he filled in the paper form with my name, address, age, telephone number (which was a party line), the amount of my initial deposit, which was $10, my father's name, his (our) address (again), and my parents' account number. That form was put in a file and rarely, if ever, viewed again.

Let's contrast the data on that form with the world we inhabit today.

- The data was handwritten. Does anyone hand-write data as a primary data input mechanism today? Not really. The only handwriting we do as a matter of course is to quickly scribble something that looks like a signature on a pad or terminal connected to a payment network or application, typically in a retail environment.

- The data was verified by the bank manager and my father. There are no systems today that would not verify the information input into a form by checking existing records. I remember the bank manager asking my father for his account number and the bank manger writing it down. No validation, no looking at the file to ensure accuracy. Just two people talking, although I expect that the level of trust between the two of them was much higher than in any system we have built in the intervening years.

- The form (the data) was stored in a filing cabinet in the lobby of the bank branch. I am pretty sure, but not completely certain, that the filing cabinet did not have a lock on the drawers. Can you imagine that today? No physical security, and access to all files by everyone who walked into the lobby.

- The data was probably never accessed again. Data reuse was not a consideration. Today the great majority of the data created is created with reuse in mind such as for understanding the demographics of the people engaging in the activity. Reuse may also include selling the data to other firms, targeting you and others for up-sell and cross-selling activities. Reuse of data is one of the primary reasons for collecting data. Think of the reuse of data by firms that you do business with on a daily basis. I bet you can come up with nearly 100 instances of reuse in a few minutes.

- The data contained personal identifiable information (PII)—information that was pertinent and relevant to me and my father and mother. There were no safeguards or limits on it on any level. Handling data that contains PII in this manner today would be grounds for legal action against the bank. Take a quick look at the summary points for handling PII in the General Data Protection

Regulation (GDPR)[1] or the California Consumer Privacy Act (CCPA).[2] This data storage and retention protocol would be against both laws.

- The data contained financial information. Not high finance and not of interest to many people, but that record, that piece of paper, was the start of my financial life and my relationship with the global banking industry. I have had banking relationships in the US and UK. Now that I think about it, opening a bank account in London in the late 1980s was very similar to opening an account in Michigan in the late 1960s, but that is a story for another book.
- There was no backup. I can't remember if the form had multiple parts or duplicate copies, but you would think that it would. Today, we make numerous copies of data for all types of reuse, backup, analytics, and more.

In the end, I had a new banking account that contained $10. I was given a paper card that had my name, address, and balance on it. I also walked out of the bank branch on a sunny summer day with a cherry flavored Tootsie Pop and a smile from ear to ear; that I remember very clearly.

I enjoyed that transaction. I spent time with my father. I got to go into a place that almost no children went to, the bank, and even more exciting was that I got to sit in Jim's office. I was part of a conversation that was mostly about me. I was given something that I didn't have before, a bank account. I took the money that had been wadded up in the front pocket of my jeans and put it in the bank where I would receive something called interest. I wouldn't get a grasp on the concept of interest for a couple of decades, but it sounded great. I felt like I had done something new, different, exciting, and well beyond my years. And it was summer, and I got a lollipop, two of my favorite things. Do we enjoy our transactions in that same way today? I don't.

In 1953, Thomas Watson, Sr. was addressing the annual shareholder meeting of IBM. He said that the IBM team expected to sell about 5 computers, but in reality had obtained orders for 18.[3] Computers were being discussed in the late 1940s and built in the early 1950s.[4] Today, just over 70 years later, the world has changed significantly. The Cubs have won a World Series, humankind has been to the Moon, Mars, Saturn, Uranus, Venus, Pluto, and beyond. The internet has been created and connected not only to the global computer infrastructure, but to all of us as well.

Computers are in the hands of the majority of the population in the developed world and many in the developing world as well. We call the devices that we carry "devices," but have you noticed that we spend the least amount of time engaged with our devices on voice calls. When I evaluate my device for functionality, the capability

---

[1] General Data Protection Regulation, https://en.wikipedia.org/wiki/General_Data_Protection_Regulation.

[2] California Consumer Privacy Act, https://en.wikipedia.org/wiki/California_Consumer_Privacy_Act.

[3] Fred Shapiro, "Our Daily Bleg: Did I.B.M. Really See a World Market 'For About Five Computers'?" *Freakonomics*, April 17, 2008, https://freakonomics.com/2008/04/17/our-daily-bleg-did-ibm-really-see-a-world-market-for-about-five-computers/.

[4] "The ILLIAC I (Illinois Automatic Computer), a pioneering computer in the ILLIAC series of computers built in 1952 by the University of Illinois, was the first computer built and owned entirely by a United States educational institution." "ILLIAC I," *Wikipedia*, https://en.wikipedia.org/wiki/ILLIAC_I.

that is the least developed, least reliable, and least enjoyable to use is the voice or call function. I will refer to our devices as *devices, computers, handhelds,* and other terms. For clarity and understanding, I am referring to the devices that we carry with us at all times.

It is not widely known, but even when you are not using your device, it is generating data about you, your location, your engagement with the world, and the engagement of the world with your device. Are you aware that even if your device is not in your hand and you are not using the device, it is receiving messages, data, and other streams of information that can be used to analyze where you are, what you are doing, and where you are moving to next?

It is not just when you are actively buying, browsing, reading, viewing, posting, and liking online that your device is actively engaged with the world around you and the companies that you have granted permissions to. You are creating data while you sleep, walk, talk, attend a school play, and go to the store to buy bread. You and your device are generating data *all* of the time. You and your device are creating data constantly and consistently.

If you have used the internet and the World Wide Web for browsing information, comparing information sources, booking travel reservations, posting to social media sites, buying and or selling new or used products of any type, running a business, or for any other purpose that can be conceived either via a computer, mobile device, or connected smart device, this book is meant for you.

One of my primary objectives in this book is to illustrate and communicate how you and your device fit into the world of data—to help you understand the entirety of the world of data that you actively participate in each and every second of each day. I want to help you and your loved ones make decisions that are right for you at this time, and as time and situations change, you can make subsequent decisions that continue to be right for you and your family.

I want you to be as informed as possible. Information and data are power, especially in the world we live in today and the world that your children will inhabit. People are collecting data and creating data about you without your knowledge or consent. I want you to understand that you have the power to change that. Data collection, data manipulation, and algorithmic amplification are not foregone conclusions. They are parts of the current environment, but this can change, and you can change your relationship, and that of your family, to data.

Some people simply do not care if they are tracked, logged, analyzed, targeted, profiled, and messaged to on a constant basis in a biased manner. That is your choice and decision. I am ok with your decision, if you are making it in an informed and aware manner.

Some people are uneasy with any data being collected about them. They are unhappy that companies, governments, associations, and others know more about their habits than they do. This group of people, once they are fully aware of their role and place in the data ecosystem, can make informed choices about permissions, data sharing, data monetization, and more.

I am not here to prescribe the right choices for you. I am here to make certain that you are informed, aware, armed, and protected from the people who would undertake actions that are counter to what you believe to be right for you, personally, your children, your family, and the people that you care about and love.

My experience and expertise through over 37 years of involvement in the field of data and analytics is being communicated in this book to help each and every one to understand their role in the data ecosystem. As noted earlier, and I want to reiterate this point—your choices are yours; I am not here to judge or to prescribe. I want to share my experience as a data and analytics professional. Over the past nearly four decades, I have been part of teams that have built over 60 different data and analytics applications that have been put into production in over 20 different industries. My work, and that of those teams, has been implemented in the UK, Western Europe, Japan, Brazil, Australia, Canada, and across the United States. I have worked for Dell, IBM, numerous technology startups, the second-largest biopharmaceutical company, global consultancies, and I have had my own management consulting firm.

I want to share my experience as a husband and father. I know what is right for me. My wife and I have collaborated to determine what is right for us and our children. Personally, I do not share any information that I do not have to. I opt out of everything possible. I block every call and text that comes to my mobile device from parties that I do not know and do not want to interact with. I call companies and have them take me and my wife off mailing lists and telephone call lists. I am on every Do Not Call and Do Not Mail list that I can register with. It works. Opting out, unsubscribing, calling, and demanding that companies stop mailing, texting, calling, and messaging does work.

I have not quantified the results, but only one or two pieces of physical mail come to our house each day. The number of unsolicited messages and calls I receive on my device each week is less than 10. As for email, I work toward a zero-in-box policy, and I am usually down to two or three e-mails at the end of each work week.

Let's be clear, I am no Luddite. I am not a recluse. I use all the modern conveniences that make my life better. When it benefits me or where I can see a benefit, I share my data. Where I have to share data to facilitate membership or to complete a transaction, I share the relevant data. I make a calculation each and every time that I am asked to share data. I ask myself, is this activity or company something that I want to be involved in? Do I want to grant them access to me? The great thing about the world we live in is that if you give them access and you decide later that it is not worth it, you can opt out.

The mission and journey that we will be undertaking in this book is to help you understand your role in taking control of your data and of how organizations collect, manipulate, manage, and leverage data about you and your family. I look forward to your input, ideas, and our future discussions. I hope you enjoy the writing and find this book useful for you and your family.

liveBook discussion forum

Purchase of *Data for All* includes free access to liveBook, Manning's online reading platform. Using liveBook's exclusive discussion features, you can attach comments to the book globally or to specific sections or paragraphs. It's a snap to make notes for yourself, ask and answer technical questions, and receive help from the author and other users. To access the forum, go to https://livebook.manning.com/book/data-for-all/discussion. You can also learn more about Manning's forums and the rules of conduct at https://livebook.manning.com/discussion.

Manning's commitment to our readers is to provide a venue where a meaningful dialogue between individual readers and between readers and the author can take place. It is not a commitment to any specific amount of participation on the part of the author, whose contribution to the forum remains voluntary (and unpaid). We suggest you try asking the author some challenging questions lest his interest stray! The forum and the archives of previous discussions will be accessible from the publisher's website as long as the book is in print.

about the author

JOHN K. THOMPSON is an international technology executive with over 37 years of experience in the fields of data, advanced analytics, and artificial intelligence (AI). John is responsible for the global AI strategy and team at EY. Prior to EY, John was responsible for the global advanced analytics and AI function at a leading biopharmaceutical company. He was an executive partner at Gartner, where he was a management consultant to market-leading companies in the areas of digital transformation, data monetization, and advanced analytics. Before Gartner, John was responsible for the advanced analytics business unit of the Dell Software Group. John is the author of the best-selling book, *Building Analytics Teams: Harnessing analytics and artificial intelligence for business improvement.* He is also co-author of the bestselling book, *Analytics: How to win with Intelligence.* John holds a bachelor of science degree in computer science from Ferris State University and an MBA in marketing from DePaul University.

The technical editor for this book, **GABOR GOLLNHOFER**, has more than 25 years of experience in data system architecture and design, data modeling, and metadata management. He has been involved in projects in finance, insurance, telecommunication, higher education, and retail industries. Currently he is the owner and managing director of a boutique company doing data-related consulting. He has worked for KPMG as manager of knowledge management and held management positions for different IT development companies. Gabor is a frequent presenter in data-related conferences and has lectured on related topics.

about the cover illustration

The images on the cover of *Data for All* are by British satirical artist John Lewis Marks (1769–1832), and are titled "The Young Fisherman" and "The Little Market Lass."

In those days, it was easy to identify where people lived and what their trade or station in life was just by their dress. Manning celebrates the inventiveness and initiative of the computer business with book covers based on the rich diversity of regional culture centuries ago, brought back to life by pictures from collections such as this one.

A history of data

This chapter covers

- What occurs as we create data through our online and offline actions
- The ramifications and implications of creating data that we do not control
- How the current data ecosystem originated
- Why we do not understand the true nature of data ownership
- A review of inaccurate descriptions of the primary characteristics of data

The path of least resistance is rarely the path of wisdom.[1]

—Tim Cook

Digital data was a minor and relatively static component in our parents' and grandparents' lives. Almost no attention was paid to it, and rightly so. Data was local, relatively static, and was not easily shared. There was almost no infrastructure to share data between individuals or companies and even less interest in collecting,

---

[1] Justin Bariso, "Tim Cook May Have Just Ended Facebook. Looks like it's no more Mr. Nice Guy," *Inc.*, January 30, 2021, https://www.inc.com/justin-bariso/tim-cook-may-have-just-ended-facebook.html.

analyzing, and leveraging data—the tools for managing and integrating data were, for the most part, paper based.

Today, digital data is a ubiquitous element in our lives. Our ability to create, store, integrate, manage, analyze, and leverage it has been transformed dramatically. Data about almost every individual and each online action taken is collected constantly and consistently.

What has not changed are the general public's views about data. This is the primary reason that motivated me to write this book: we, as individuals, need to change our views on data.

In this book we will look at the opportunities available to all of us to protect, manage, own, and monetize our own data. Let's begin our discussion.

1.1   *A concerning situation*

Most people don't think about the repercussions of simply sending a picture or a file. They think, "I just sent a picture to my friend. What's the big deal?" Yes, it's true that you took a picture, recorded a video, or captured a silly audio snippet and sent it to the intended recipient. That is one thing that happened, but that is not the extent of what happened.

Let's take a step back and look at the process that occurs when you record and send a piece of media over the internet; it may well change your willingness to send pictures, messages, and videos so casually.

1.1.1   *Life cycle of a video, picture, text, email, or file*

First, you recorded the video on your device. Even if you "delete" it, you only delete the pointer to the file or video, not the file itself. The file may be marked for future deletion, and if you need storage space, your device might overwrite it with a new picture, video, or audio, but that is not likely as modern devices have more storage than most people use. So that file will probably remain on your device, even when you repurpose or trade-in your device for a new one.

When you share the file, it is sent to the internet via a network. This might be your mobile device network (a telephone network). It might be via a Wi-Fi network that you were connected to when you sat in a coffee shop, a plane, a train, the back seat of a car, or while you walked down the street.

Once the file is sent, the backbone servers of the internet send it and the routing information across multiple servers, routers, and telecommunication providers until it arrives on the device of the intended recipient. Some of the servers and all the routers will log their activity. The logs contain, at the very least, the sender's device identifier, the filename, the size of the file, and the receiver's device identifier. Yes, the core infrastructure of the network that was traversed does not store the content of the file, but the existence of the file, the date and time it was sent and received, and the size and type of the file are stored, possibly forever.

That is the life cycle of a data file. It's not just on your device. It is everywhere now.

1.1.2   All your online actions create permanent records of your activity

An analytics professional, like myself, does not need the file's content to prove that you were part of the process of recording and sending that file. If you sent something that you might be embarrassed about, or that is illegal or unethical, you have made a permanent record of your actions that can be resurrected at any time in the future, and probably will be when you least want it to be remembered. But that is not the most concerning part of this scenario.

I mentioned the routers and the network infrastructure of the internet in passing, but we need to talk a bit more about the servers. The servers *do* make copies of the files—the actual content that you recorded, stored, and sent—and the earlier description of how a delete operation works on your device also applies to those numerous servers.

More than likely, your file will be deleted and overwritten relatively quickly due to the amount of traffic that traverses those servers, but those servers are backed up. Backup copies are made and archived. If your file was on the server when the backup was executed, then your file has an infinite lifetime. To make matters worse, your file traveled to and through multiple servers. The chances of all copies being deleted and none being backed up and retained is nil, zilch, zero. That file, and all the information about when you recorded it, sent it, and who received and possibly forwarded it with additional commentary is now ensconced in the digital library of the world in perpetuity.

Are you comfortable with all of your pictures, videos, tweets, texts, commentary, snarky remarks, and petty comments being preserved for all time? Are you comfortable that your children are making good choices every time they record and send something to a friend or acquaintance? Are you aware of and in control of every action that you, your partner or spouse, your children, mother, father, aunts, uncles, employees, coworkers, confidants, and acquaintances take each and every minute of every day?

1.1.3   Intelligent choices

The best we can do is be armed with knowledge and understand the possible ramifications of our actions, the implications of the lifespan of the data we are creating each and every minute of every day, and the potential for that data to be misused and abused once it is beyond our grasp and control.

Once we have amassed that knowledge, we can make good choices and teach our children to make good choices. We can lead by example for all to see. We can be intelligent about our actions, about the data we create through our actions, and about the data we choose to record and share in any and all electronic forms.

You are not responsible for everyone you know and are related to. It is not up to you to help them to make the best possible choices. But by not taking that compromising photo; by not documenting a truly unfortunate perspective and documenting it in a video, post, or text; by avoiding a link that would make you a ransomware victim and make your laptop a new host that continues to propagate a malware attack, you are leading by example. You are making intelligent choices. Intelligent choices by each individual help build and maintain a civil society.

That is not hyperbole or overreach. Each of us is responsible for our data and for the life cycle of our data. Whether we have ever thought about it or not, it is up to us to take control of our data and to actively make conscious choices about how our data is stored, managed, and used. Each of us has a duty to the people we care about to help them understand the implications of their everyday actions and the implications of the data they create as byproducts of their actions, such as these:

- Walking down a street in Chicago or London. You may or may not know that Chicago and London are the cities with the highest number of video surveillance cameras viewing city streets on a 24-hour, 7 day a week, basis.
- Browsing websites that espouse discredited theories and lies about any number of people or topics.
- Taking photographs of ourselves, or parts of ourselves or others, that could prove to be incriminating or embarrassing.

Before you started reading this book, you may not have believed that you are at the center of managing and controlling your data. That lack of awareness, so far, has not been a personal failing. But if you persist in being oblivious to what is happening to your data with your implicit, and in many cases explicit, consent, then it is your fault. You are complicit in enabling the misuse and abuse of your data, your identity, your attention, your credit scores, and your reputation.

The data ecosystem was never intended to become what it is today. It has organically and rapidly evolved over the past 30 years into a global system of data creation and use due to the independent actions of corporations, governments, and individuals. These millions of entities are acting on their own best, narrowly defined, interests. No one is driving the bus, and that needs to change.

To participate in this ecosystem, each of us is required to sign agreements—if we don't agree, we can't participate. But even with that hard and fast requirement, we should read and understand what we are agreeing to. Sometimes there is a choice, and that is a discussion for another part of this book. But we are making uninformed choices. We need to understand the extent of what the company intends to do with our data and which companies and governments they are sharing it with, in your country and around the world. That decision has far reaching ramifications for you and all of society.

Let's explore one example of this for clarification.

1.2   *An example: Genetic testing and reporting*

There are a number of private companies that offer genetic testing, ostensibly for genealogy purposes. The appeal is obvious. Where did my family come from? Who are my ancestors? Are the stories I've been told about my family plausible based on my genetic make-up?

People are curious, and knowing can provide great comfort to many. But we are not concerned here with comfort and curiosity about family trees, epochs of human migration, or other related topics. Here and now, we are focused on what happens to your genetic information once you provide that swab to the vendor.

1.2.1   Genetic sequencing

The vendor takes your sample and loads it into a sequencing machine, where the sample is decomposed into hundreds of millions of fragments, which are all stored in your personal library. Each fragment is copied millions of times, and the millions of fragments are read and analyzed to understand how each fragment fits into your genome or into the structure of your DNA. As it says on the shampoo bottle, rinse and repeat, millions of times, until the DNA sequencer has built a complete picture of who you are, from the perspective of your DNA.

DEIDENTIFYING DATA

I was talking with a group of professionals about deidentifying DNA data. The organization that was storing and managing the data was stripping off the names, addresses, and other data elements such as age, gender, and weight. The company representatives were satisfied that they had met the legal burden for deidentifying the data records.

In my opinion, and that of other data professionals on the call, the company *had* met the legal burden, but this was DNA data. A complete genome is the ultimate personal identifier, isn't it? It is impossible to truly deidentify your complete genome.

The data professionals politely smiled until someone pointed out this flaw in their approach. The lawyer on the call asked, "but have we met the legal burden imposed on the company?" We all agreed that they had. The discussion ended on a note of mixed emotions.

YOUR GENETIC DATA IS NOW FOR SALE ON THE GENERAL MARKET

How can those genetic testing companies make money from providing you a report about the probability of where your genetic material came from? They can't. Genetic testing, sequencing, and providing reports to individuals is not a viable business model. There are not enough people willing to pay for the service to make these companies ongoing, profitable organizations. The cost of genetic testing and reporting by a consumer-oriented company is between $60 and $150.

"By the start of 2019, more than 26 million consumers had added their DNA to four leading commercial ancestry and health databases, according to . . . estimates."[2] These companies began by representing that they were not intending to share your genetic data with third parties. They represented that when you submitted your swab and your genome was analyzed that only the company and you would have access to the data.

---

[2] Antonio Regalado, "More than 26 million people have taken an at-home ancestry test," *MIT Technology Review*, February 11, 2019, https://www.technologyreview.com/2019/02/11/103446/more-than-26-million-people-have-taken-an-at-home-ancestry-test/.

> *During the summer [of 2019], the big four big ancestry companies all promised they wouldn't let police into their databases without a warrant. But it was only weeks before the smallest player, Family Tree DNA, changed its mind and began allowing the FBI to upload DNA from corpses or blood spatters and surf the database just like any other customer, checking out names and who is related to who.*[3]

The vast majority of these companies began with investments from venture capital firms and private equity firms. The founding management teams who wrote the original policies that govern what happens to your data work at the pleasure of the venture partners who are in control of the boards of directors. Venture capital firms are not well known for protecting the data security and privacy of people who have signed up for services from one of their portfolio firms. When management changes, so do objectives: they pivot to new business models, they change their terms of service, they rewrite their privacy policies.

So when you sign up for a service and provide your swab with your DNA sample, the DNA firm you signed up with does not control your resulting data. The policies they originally posted mean little to nothing and can be changed at any time, sometimes without notifying you.

In this example, the people providing DNA samples to companies offering genealogy-related services are basically posting their DNA to an open forum where any governmental agency or private company, including insurance companies, can gain access to their data for a relatively small fee. This is a possible abuse of private data that you should be very concerned about.

Genetic data is unique in that it is the code that defines our individual make-up, but genetic data is just one type of data among the thousands of types we create and send out into the world each day. All of us need to start thinking about how we can protect and control our data before we hand it over to external parties.

To close out this aspect of our discussion, think about the point made in the following quote:

> *"[The] first rule of data: once you hand it over, you lose control of it. You have no idea how the terms of service will change for your 'recreational' DNA sample," tweeted Elizabeth Joh, a law professor at the University of California, Davis.*[4]

1.3   *The beginnings of modern data*

Let's look back at the evolution of data to see when data became a recognizable and distinct element and topic. We'll look at how data was handled in the 1920s and see how those processes set a precedent that we are subject to today; by looking at the past, we can understand how we got to where we are now.

---

[3] Ibid.
[4] Ibid.

1.3.1   *Commercial data and analytics: Data as a valuable commodity*

The data world of today was shaped and originated, in large part, in Chicago. ACNielsen, Information Resources Inc. (IRI), comScore, comPysch, efficient market services (ems), Market6, and SPINS are just a few of the companies that created the foundation of how Americans think (or don't think) about syndicated data, market research data, personal data, purchasing data, and the wide range of data that we create daily but are, for the most part, oblivious to.

These companies and their actions created the societal, legal, and governmental framework that we consider the "norm" in how we enable others to use our data. They did it without our active involvement, consent, or even scant level of understanding of what was happening with our data.

Arthur C. Nielsen, an entrepreneur and engineer from the Chicago area, is widely considered the founder of market research:

> *Arthur founded the ACNielsen company in 1923, and in doing so advanced the new field of market research. This involved: (1.) test marketing new products to determine their viability prior to costly mass marketing and production; and (2.) measuring product sales at a random sample of stores to determine market share.*[5]

Many of the terms and attitudes relating to data can be traced back to Nielsen.

The work of Arthur Nielsen and his company was innovative for the early 1920s, but the important thing for us to consider is that over time the ACNielsen company convinced the grocery store operators to provide, at no cost, or at a very low cost, to his company, all of the sales records from each and every one of their stores. By collecting data primarily for analysis and for reselling the raw data and related intelligence to companies and individuals, Nielsen set in motion an entirely new asset class and new industry. This innovation marks the beginning of data as a unique and valuable commercial commodity. Data as an asset unto itself began in this moment.

The next step in the evolution of the industry involved the first generation of data brokers, like InfoUSA and other firms that worked predominantly in the direct mail industry. The second generation of data brokers included Experian, Acxiom, and Epsilon. These three firms are mostly known in the arena of credit scores and determining the credit worthiness of individuals. Today we have a third generation of data brokers who are focused on collecting information from online activities, including location data, browsing behavior, and purchasing.

Starting with Nielsen, entire industries handed over the keys to the kingdom, their data, without so much as a significant discussion about the power shift that would take place. This transfer of data from one industry to another without requisite consideration and compensation suggested that data was not valuable and did not need to be valued. The precedent set in this instance is that as data ownership has almost no value, it can be transferred from individuals to companies without the consent of the individuals who created the data. This precedent of devaluing data and relegating

---

[5] "Arthur Nielsen," *Wikipedia*, https://en.wikipedia.org/wiki/Arthur_Nielsen.

data to the status of a meaningless commodity is at the core of the situation we find ourselves in today as it relates to data.

1.3.2 *How our data rights and right to compensation were diverted*

The asymmetrical relationship that this initial inter-industry agreement and transfer created, and the data framework that evolved from it, shows a direct line from this first transfer to the relationships we are bound by in our agreements with online platforms, social media companies, and other corporations.

I started in the analytics business in 1989, and for the first 10 years or so I focused on consumer-packaged goods (CPG) companies, known in the UK as fast moving consumer goods (FMCG) companies. The entire industry used scanner and panel data for much of the tactical and strategic analytics we developed. I was stunned to learn that data was given to them, for low to no cost, by the grocery retailers via ACNielsen and IRI.

No one could explain, at the time, why the retailers simply gave up their data, but a common disclaimer was, "It is just sales data anyway, it isn't worth much." Today the response to the same question is that people do not care what happens to their data, they just want free email.

But just because a handful of grocery store owners and operators did not appreciate the value of data as an asset in 1923, do we need to continue on this path of disempowerment? I don't think that we do.

1.3.3 *Let's jump forward to the late 20th century . . . in the UK*

Clive Humby and Edwina Dunn of dunnHumby have been involved in analytics in the UK since 1976. They, like ACNielsen, focused their efforts on the FMCG and retail industries, and on loyalty and pricing. Their company was purchased by Tesco, the UK retailer, in 2011.

> *In 2006, Humby coined the phrase "Data is the new oil." Michael Palmer expanded on Humby's quote by saying, like oil, data is "valuable, but if unrefined it cannot really be used. Oil has to be changed into gas, plastic, chemicals, etc. to create a valuable entity that drives profitable activity; so, data must be broken down and analysed for it to have value."*[6]

Dunn retorted, "The phrase (Data is the new oil) has since become something of a corporate cliché, uttered by every consultant and CEO who wants to be seen to understand the digital economy."[7]

In 1998, Google was founded. This was one of the first instances of consumers obtaining a free online service in exchange for the company's unfettered use of data that the users themselves created. The first free service from Google was search. With Google, users had, and still have, the ability to search for anything on the then relatively new World Wide Web (WWW). The WWW was exploding with content, companies,

---

[6] "Clive Humby," *Wikipedia*, https://en.wikipedia.org/wiki/Clive_Humby.

[7] Josh Sims, "Is data democratization really a good idea?" *Raconteur*, September 19, 2021, https://www.raconteur .net/technology/data-analytics/is-data-democratisation-a-good-idea-really/.

products, services, movements, research, organizations, hobbies, and groups. People reacted very positively to this new free service—uptake was rapid and engagement remains high.

In 2021, Google remains by far the most popular search engine. According to Reliablesoft, the ten best search engines in 2021, ranked by popularity, are Google, Microsoft Bing, Yahoo, Baidu, Yandex, DuckDuckGo, Ask.com, Ecosia, Aol.com, and Internet Archive.[8] Figure 1.1 illustrates the incredible global market share still held by Google. Some sources put Google's market share in excess of 90%.[9]

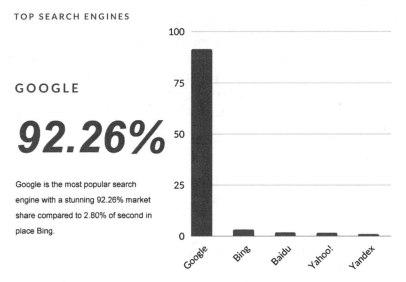

TOP SEARCH ENGINES

GOOGLE

92.26%

Google is the most popular search engine with a stunning 92.26% market share compared to 2.80% of second in place Bing.

Figure 1.1   Global search engine market share. Source: Reliablesoft (https://www.reliablesoft.net/top-10-search-engines-in-the-world/)

Shortly after the release of Google's search service, the founders reacted in a spectacularly unimaginative manner by deciding that their business model would be advertising-based. Technologically, Google is an interesting company, but from a business model perspective, they are about as dull as dishwater, because venture capitalists and financial analysts prefer stability and predictability in business operations.

Arthur Nielsen founded his firm 70 years ago by gaining free access to sales data and analyzing how companies could sell more groceries to people through more targeted and refined pricing, better store assortments, and shelf-space optimization. That ultimately led to targeting of radio and television advertising. Today we are offered virtually the same thing on our computers over the internet with little to no change in the underlying premise. Consumers or intermediaries (e.g., grocery stores,

---

[8] Alex Chris, Top 10 Search Engines in the World (2021 Update), Reliablesoft, September 9, 2021, https://www.reliablesoft.net/top-10-search-engines-in-the-world/.

[9] Thomas J Law, December 11, 2020, MEET THE TOP 10 SEARCH ENGINES IN THE WORLD IN 2021, Oberlo, https://www.oberlo.com/blog/top-search-engines-world.

radio stations, and televisions stations) provide our data for free, and CPG and FMCG companies use it to sell us more products and services. To them, we remain the commodity to be sold, through our data.

Of course, now the medium is different. The internet and the World Wide Web are not Tesco, Marks and Spencer, Jewel, or Piggly Wiggly, but the business model is exactly the same. CPG and FMCG companies get our data for free and sell us more things. They get to formulate messages and target them to induce us to buy items that we do not need or really want, and to make us feel rage and anger to separate us from our fellow citizens.

ACNielsen started with grocery stores and expanded into intelligence for targeting advertising in newspapers, radio, and television. Google took this same model and applied it to the newly emerging online world. Google had an opportunity to make something new, interesting, and innovative, but they chose to refine a model that concentrates money and power in the hands of the few. Truly, a once in a lifetime opportunity, lost to a lack of vision. This brings us to the twenty-first century where we find ourselves today.

1.4   *Modern data in the present day*

The rights of individuals to own, protect, manage, and monetize their own data has been usurped by a past that has little to no relevance to the data ecosystem we have today. Companies around the world have acted like they own our data. That is not true, and it is a temporary situation that will change in the near future. Let's examine where we are today in relation to our data rights, our data ownership, and our ability to monetize our data.

1.4.1   *The dangers of social media*

Facebook was founded in 2004. In 2018, after the Cambridge Analytica scandal, NYU professor Scott Galloway called the founder, "the most dangerous person in the world."[10] His lack of care for humanity and his zeal for destroying civil society is unrivaled.

Galloway later stated, "There's a firm that's grown faster than any firm to date. Its founder also set the DNA of the firm, but without the benefit of the modulation and self-awareness that come(s) with age. It's in a sector where network effects created a handful of organisms of unprecedented scale. There has never been an organization of this scale and influence, that is more like its founder, than Facebook."[11]

"Facebook and other social media companies describe themselves as neutral platforms," Jeff Bewkes, former CEO of Time Warner, said, "but their product is not a

---

[10]Chloe Aiello, "Mark Zuckerberg is the most 'powerful, dangerous person in the world': NYU's Scott Galloway," *CNBC*, May 11, 2018, https://www.cnbc.com/2018/05/11/nyus-scott-galloway-zuckerberg-is-the-most-dangerous-person-in-the-world.html.

[11]Scott Galloway, "Facebook reinforces the power and influence of sociopaths," *Business Insider*, originally published on May 31, 2019, republished on September 24, 2021, https://www.businessinsider.com/scott-galloway-facebook-influence-sociopath-power-2021-9.

neutral presentation of user-provided content. It's an actively managed feed, personalized for each user, and boosting some pieces exponentially more than other pieces of content."[12]

Facebook has taken what Google started in the online world and has weaponized the data that we continue to create in dangerous new ways. Facebook is one of the most aggressive firms in using artificial intelligence (AI), machine learning (ML), and a wide range of resources and algorithms to amplify signals that evoke negative and violent thoughts and actions from people.

1.4.2 People are waking up to the abuse of our data

In 2021, Frances Haugen came forward as a whistleblower after working at Facebook for two years. Her testimony before the US Senate, on television and radio, in newspaper stories, and in podcasts focused on how Facebook uses data to understand the negative affect it is having on its users and on how Facebook prioritizes profits and growth over the wellbeing of those who use its online properties.

Her testimony revealed that Facebook coveted young users, despite health concerns. Lawmakers were particularly concerned about the affect of Instagram. Haugen leaked one Facebook study that found that 13.5% of UK teen girls said their suicidal thoughts became more frequent after starting on Instagram. Another leaked study found 17% of teen girls said their eating disorders got worse after using Instagram."[13] Facebook's researchers found that about 32% of teen girls said that when they felt bad about their bodies, Instagram made them feel worse, which was first reported by the *Wall Street Journal.*

Senator Marsha Blackburn (R-Tenn.) accused Facebook of intentionally targeting children under age 13 with an "addictive" product, despite the app requiring users to be 13 years or older. Facebook's reaction was predictable. They argued that the research was taken out of context and that Facebook does care about users over profit.

1.4.3 And here we find ourselves

Over the past 100 years we have moved on from the beginning and early stages of commercially collecting, cleaning, integrating, aggregating, analyzing, packaging, and using data to understand and influence human behavior on a large scale and widespread basis.

The early founders of the data and analytics industry, like Arthur Nielsen, Danny Moore, and Wayne Levy, moved slowly at first, seeking to make money by selling insights on how to sell more household consumable goods. In the 1990s, analytics professionals were very careful to work on analytics that would help companies understand buyer behavior, assiduously avoiding unethical use cases. Today, these use cases that focused on selling products based on actual product characteristics and known

---

[12]Scott Galloway, "No Mercy, No Malice, Facebook . . . what to do?" November 5, 2021, https://www.profgalloway .com/facebook-what-to-do/.

[13]Bobby Allyn, "Here are 4 key points from the Facebook whistleblower's testimony on Capitol Hill," *NPR*, Oct. 5, 2021, https://www.npr.org/2021/10/05/1043377310/facebook-whistleblower-frances-haugen-congress.

benefits, and the early commercial use of data, look quaint and even valuable to not only the companies producing the products, but also to the consumers who may want and need these products and services.

Today, the ability to target content, messaging, products, and services is considered by many companies, individuals, and governments to be a "meets minimum" capability. In 2021, global advertising spend was over $763 billion (as shown in figure 1.2).[14] It is obvious that advertising is here to stay and that the use of data to refine and target advertising will not be diminishing in the foreseeable future. Data is the key to the advertising industry, as it has become a key raw material in numerous industries, including finance and insurance, automotive, pharmaceuticals, CPG/FMCG, retail, and many others.

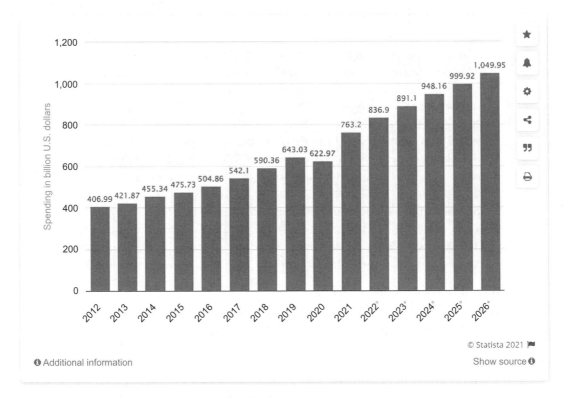

Figure 1.2   Global advertising revenue 2012–2026 (Statista, https://www.statista.com/statistics/236943/global-advertising-spending/)

The proliferation and use of data will not abate anytime soon, and I am not writing this book to call for a reduction in the use of data; quite the opposite. My professional career and interests are firmly rooted in the widespread use of data and analytics.

---

[14]A. Guttmann, Global advertising revenue 2012–2026, *Statista,* Dec 7, 2021, https://www.statista.com/statistics/236943/global-advertising-spending/.

Now that you have a better understanding of the genesis of the data industry, you'll have a deeper appreciation of the possible future of data for all of us. The past of data should *not* be the future of data.

1.5   The new and current view and value of data

While data is not at the top of mind for many people, it is on the minds of many leading thinkers and governments. That is a good thing. Change only comes to society as a whole when the society's leaders are thinking and talking about a needed and intended change. Leading thinkers are casting about for a new definition of the view, value, and salient characteristics of data.

I hesitate to say that data is a ubiquitous commodity because I believe that labeling data as a commodity downplays the importance of the role data exerts in our world on an individual and collective level. There are commentators aplenty, however, working diligently to label data as the new fill-in-the-blank. We already called out Clive Humby for his "Data is the new oil" remark. Here are a few of the other "data is the new ____" analogies.

1.5.1   Data is the new sand

In his article "*Data Is the New Sand,*" Tim O'Reilly remarked:

> *The ownership issue with user data is not value. It is control. Does the individual or the company that collects data have the right to control what is collected and how it is used? Does the company have an obligation to use the data that it acquires about users only for their benefit, or is it free to use it against them? Is it free to treat it as an asset to be resold without any incremental benefit to the user from whom it was collected?[15]*

O'Reilly postulates that our individual data is not that valuable and that it is like sand—ubiquitous and requiring much processing to make it valuable to firms and ultimately to us in the form of targeted messaging and advertising.

To make his point, O'Reilly brings forth another comparison:

> *Data is the new Oxycontin. Like an opioid, data is highly addictive and dangerous when overprescribed, but extremely useful when prescribed correctly. It is harmful when companies turn it against their users to enhance their profits or competitive position, but beneficial when it is used on behalf of the people from whom it is collected.[16]*

O'Reilly makes the point about control of data, but I am not aware of any of his writings expounding on the possibility of the social good of the control of data moving back to the individual. It must be said that his business is rooted in publishing. I expect that he has a conflict of interest in enabling each user and individual to control and monetize their own data to maximize their own benefit.

However, I agree with Tim O'Reilly's overall point, and the question remains, can we trust any and all organizations to use our data in a way that is aligned with our values,

---

[15]Tim O'Reilly, "Data Is the New Sand," *The Information,* Feb. 24, 2021, https://www.theinformation.com/articles/data-is-the-new-sand.
[16]Ibid.

interests, and desires, and those of our children, parents, friends, communities, countries, and the planet?

1.5.2   Data is the new sun

Bill Schmarzo, an educator and data management customer advocate for Dell Technologies, compares data to the sun in his recent posts, articles, and remarks:

> *Data is the New Sun is a more relevant analogy . . . as the sun can power an infinite number of uses at zero marginal cost, never wears out (or depreciates) and never depletes! At its heart, digital transformation is about economics: transitioning from yesterday's "economics of oil" mentality (expensive to find, expensive to extract, expensive to transport, environmentally hazardous, depletes, messy, dirty, and environmental costly) to embracing the modern "economics of the sun" (clean, never depletes, never depreciates and is readily available to fuel an infinite number of uses).[17]*

I find the premise of this analogy compelling. If you need an analogy, this is a good one to use. The Sun will eventually deplete, and it will wear out, but for our immediate purposes, this analogy works for now.

1.5.3   Data is the new gold

Tshilidzi Marwala, professor, vice-chancellor, and principal of the University of Johannesburg, said:

> *The most valuable asset of Uber, the ride-hailing service . . . is the data of the people who use it. The prime asset of Google, the largest library, which owns no physical library, is the index that takes customers to their desired websites. Therefore, the new valuable asset is not gold, but it is data. Data has become the new gold![18]*

Marwala's logic and arguments are solid and based in reality, but I do think they are limited in past historical thinking and are too limiting to the prospects of data.

1.5.4   Data is the new currency

Jane Barratt, chief advocacy officer for MX Technologies, commented in a recent podcast,

> *It is still very early days in this data-as-currency world, but it is an absolutely one-sided trade. The buyers at this point are amassing, assessing, consolidating data, and then using it. They are the ones that can put data to work in the economic model. The generators of data are basically getting nothing. Think about a social media platform that says, "Our user is worth $120 to us in the course of a year." To you, it seems like a decent trade. You think, "Okay, they give me photos, help me keep in touch with family," and so on. Then you realize that this amount is aggregated across the world. If you're looking at a New York City-based person who is earning half a million dollars a year, of course they're worth more from an advertising model and a monetization model than someone in a village in an emerging market.[19]*

[17] Bill Schmarzo, "It's About Economics! Data is the New Sun," *LinkedIn* post, Sept. 18, 2017, https://www.linkedin.com/pulse/its-economics-data-new-sun-bill-schmarzo/.

[18] Tshilidzi Marwala, "Data Is the New Gold," *Forbes Africa,* July 18, 2019, https://www.forbesafrica.com/technology/2019/07/18/data-is-the-new-gold/.

[19] Jane Barratt, August 27, 2019, Knowledge at Wharton podcast series, Data as Currency: What Value Are You Getting for It?, https://knowledge.wharton.upenn.edu/article/barrett-data-as-currency/.

We have seen the first commercial data exchange opened in China.[20] Data exchanges, like stock exchanges, are where people and companies will congregate, virtually, to offer, buy, and sell data in an open market. We will see more data exchanges open around the world.

We will also see data commons begin to be established, mainly by national and regional governments, like the European Union. Data commons are a very exciting prospect. They are now being defined, and laws are being drafted to govern them. Data commons can and will be one of the paths toward individuals controlling and monetizing their own data for their benefit.

Data will be considered a currency in the future, but we are not there just yet.

1.5.5 *Data is the new plastic*

Ved Sen, head of business innovation in the UK and Ireland for Tata Consultancy Services, describes data as "the new plastic," because "we create a lot, we struggle to know what to do with it and it tends to turn up in the wrong places. And, for all the talk about the democratization of data, business is not yet culturally geared up to handle this. There's a lot to do."[21]

Sen's analogy is a bit dark and depressing for me, but there are elements of truth in his view. It is not for me, personally.

1.5.6 *Data is the new bacon*

To add a little levity, Paul Brouwers says, "According to Google, [data] is therefore one of the following: Oil, Gold, Currency, Bacon, Future. And if I had to pick one, it might as well be bacon!"[22]

It is always a pleasant distraction when someone adds a counterpoint that is based in humor. I appreciate Brouwers' offering to the global discussion, and I really do enjoy bacon, especially on a good cheeseburger. However, I have to reject the premise that bacon is the answer in this context.

1.5.7 *Data is the new future*

Tom Davenport and Thomas C. Redman offer us the following: "It is clear enough that the future depends on data, so sooner or later, you have no real choice. As in all things, audentes Fortuna iuvat—fortune favors the brave."[23]

There are numerous other analogies, but these eight are representative of the majority of the analogies offered. It is clear that data represents the future, a potential

---

[20]Jane Barratt, "Data as Currency: What Value Are You Getting?" *Knowledge at Wharton* podcast series, Aug. 27, 2019, https://knowledge.wharton.upenn.edu/article/barrett-data-as-currency/.

[21]Shi Jing, "Shanghai launches data exchange," *China Daily*, Nov. 26, 2021, http://english.www.gov.cn/news/topnews/202111/26/content_WS61a04d80c6d0df57f98e5977.html.

[22]Paul Brouwers, "Data is the new Bacon," *Medium*, June 10, 2020, https://medium.com/@BrouwersPPM/data-is-the-new-bacon-74ab91e76e43.

[23]Tom Davenport, "Getting Serious about Data and Data Science," Oct. 5, 2020, https://www.tomdavenport.com/getting-serious-about-data-and-data-science/.

currency, a method of changing the existing power dynamic between consumers, companies, and governments, a food, and a source of humor.

For the immediate future, Bill Schmarzo and Jane Barratt seem to be the closest to the truth. The characteristics of the sun and data are closely aligned in a physical and metaphorical sense. For the longer-term future, data is a currency and a valuable and ubiquitous one at that. In the end, I believe that Davenport adds a valuable perspective to the discussion: data is the future.

1.6   *Wrapping up*

Data can provide us with a brighter future, but only if we are aware of the implications of continuing in the current mode and decide to act. Sleeping through a problem is easy, but it is not optimal to let others continue to take advantage of us. Being unaware and oblivious is comfortable, until it isn't.

The band Devo stated, "Freedom of choice is what you've got. Freedom from choice is what you want."[24] That is a disturbing thought. Letting others make our decisions seems simple and unencumbering until you have no choice.

The current model of companies collecting and using our data was built by people who do not have our best interests in mind. This can change—it does not need to be the way things are. The world of data can, should, and will change.

People should be allowed to take an active part in the management, use, and monetization of their data. Today, individuals can engage in this process, but it is disjointed, complicated, and time consuming, and most people do not see the value in engaging with the current process to limit and control their data.

This fundamental change in the world of data does not need to be adopted by a majority of the populace. As stated earlier, a group of thought leaders can effect this change. Those are the people this book is for. The people who can see, and want, change. That is not everyone; it is not even a slim majority.

This is not an altruistic endeavor. This is a capitalistic vision and operation. Forward-thinking governments have started to discuss the creation and regulation of data exchanges and data commons.[25] Companies will follow with offerings where it will be simple for every person to make choices about the use of their data. These companies will make money by enabling individuals in the process of proactively managing, controlling, sharing, and monetizing their data.

Commercial firms will be founded to manage, control, and monetize the data from each and every individual. It will be simple, and a substantial portion of the general population will participate. When this happens, the data world will shift dramatically. Power will irrevocably move from companies to individuals.

---

[24]Mark Mothersbaugh, Gerald Casale, & Devo, "Freedom of Choice" (song), 1980, discussed in the Wikipedia article, https://en.wikipedia.org/wiki/Freedom_of_Choice_(song).

[25]European Commission, "A European Strategy for data," July 2020, https://digital-strategy.ec.europa.eu/en/policies/strategy-data.

As you read this book, take the lessons and information to heart. An informed population can and will make better decisions that can effect social change. It has to happen. The arc of human history bends toward the best possible outcome for the global population. But in the current data industry, the extraction of data, its use, and its value is imbalanced and in favor of people and organizations working against the common good. This is a wrong that needs to be, and will be, corrected, by the evolution of the data industry toward a new model that delivers value to every individual.

Some people will still value free services and give their data to companies in exchange for those services. Those individuals will continue to be fodder for the misuse of their data, and they will continue to be targeted for products, services, and offerings. They might even find the targeting to be valuable and comforting.

This book is a signal of what is coming in the realm of data. There is no doubt that this future is hard to see, and many people do not agree that this will happen, but it will. When it does, a significant portion of the global population will choose to take control of their data.

Asleep no more . . . onward!

Summary

- Data has been a byproduct of human history for thousands of years.
- When data was limited in its portability, accessibility, and use, it was not a concern or consideration for most people or companies.
- As data has become ubiquitous, portable, accessible, and created by every individual online on a consistent and constant basis, the characteristics of data have changed.
- Our data rights have been temporarily usurped by companies that have extended previous laws and norms into the data ecosystem of today.
- Governments and leading thinkers are aware of the need to move data ownership back to the individual, and change is coming.
- We as individuals will soon have the right to protect, own, manage, and monetize our own data.

How data works today

2

This chapter covers
- How data is created from daily online actions and offline activities
- Where data travels and where it is stored
- How leveraging multiple sources of data increases the ability of companies to target you
- Free online services like email and apps are not truly free
- What you can begin to do to control your data

Customers need to be given control of their own data . . .[1]

—Tim Berners-Lee

How much time do you spend on your mobile device? A recent study by data.ai (née App Annie) showed that "across the top 10 markets analyzed, the weighted average surpassed 4 hours 48 minutes in 2021—up 30% from 2019. Users in Brazil, Indonesia and South Korea surpassed 5 hours per day in mobile apps in 2021. The

---

[1] Pieter Verdegem, "Tim Berners-Lee's plan to save the internet: give us back control of our data," *The Conversation*, February 5, 2021, https://theconversation.com/tim-berners-lees-plan-to-save-the-internet-give-us-back-control-of-our-data-154130.

average American watched 3.1 hours of TV a day, whereas they spent 4.1 hours on their mobile device in 2021."[2] That is a substantial amount of each person's day. Keep in mind, not only are all those individuals using apps and browsing content, but they are also generating data.

The average American has 80 apps downloaded on their phone. The average smartphone owner uses 9–10 apps per day and 30 per month, according to the staffing firm Zippia.[3] In today's data ecosystem, most of us cannot know, much less control, where data is recorded, stored, integrated, and used to analyze and target everyone.

In this chapter we will delve into the world of data as it is today. We will discuss how you create data, where it resides, and how it is processed, integrated, analyzed, shared, and used in manners that you may, or may not, agree with.

2.1 Where does data originate?

Most people are unaware of how companies use our data, but you will know after reading this book. Once you have that knowledge, you may stop, or at least modify, how you create data for those companies and which companies you want to create data for.

You may want to shop online. You might be interested in what is happening with your local bird-watching group on social media. You may think that an online payment system is the best way to buy baked goods at the local farmer's market. You may like having free email and search from Google and other providers. I am not saying that you cannot use these platforms, but we can all do a better job of managing the data we create if we use these applications and systems. We can do a better job of requesting to review, manage, and control how long the data is retained, managed, analyzed, and used. We might even want it deleted.

The most important point is that you can control your data. Do not share more than is required to complete the action at hand, whether you're purchasing a roll of paper towels, completing a survey, or acquiring a house. Controlling your data controls the downstream actions that can be targeted and reduces the influence on you and your loved ones.

Let's discuss how data is created and what happens with your data after you create it.

2.2 The life cycle of data

The data you create may be stored in the country where you created it, or it may be stored in another country with few or no laws governing what can be done with it. Companies move data to jurisdictions that give them more leeway to use your data in more aggressive ways. They copy and send it to multiple locations for use by numerous companies in many processes. We simply do not know the details of what happens after we create data.

Let's start by looking at location data.

---

[2] "State of Mobile 2022," *data.ai*, https://www.data.ai/en/go/state-of-mobile-2022.

[3] Jack Flynn, "40 fascinating mobile app industry statistics [2022]: The success of mobile apps in the U.S.," *Zippia*, Oct. 19, 2022, https://www.zippia.com/advice/mobile-app-industry-statistics/.

2.2.1   *Location services*

Location services sound simple, and they are free! Many vendors provide such services on a global basis, including your mobile phone provider, Google, Apple, Waze, Alibaba, Foursquare, HERE, Aisle411, Baidu, Dianping, NavInfo, Etisalat, Facebook, City-data, Telenav, Gravy Data, and others you have never heard of.[4] Location services are useful for finding your way to all the new locations you need to travel to, but location services are tracking your every movement down to a few feet or meters in accuracy.

Google's location service accumulates data in 260 countries and territories, from Antarctica to Vatican City.[5] Google Maps enables anyone to calculate driving, walking, or bus ride times from most locations in the world to any other location in the world.[6] These free online services are easy to use and available anywhere you can connect to the internet. Most people only think of the consumer-facing side of these services: users can arrive on time via the most efficient route through an easy-to-use online service. Very convenient.

What users rarely think about is the other side of the service: a commercial-grade data service and data access service that third-party companies pay Google to use. For the right price, anyone can buy the data and know where you've been. More importantly, you do not get paid for contributing your data to the companies that provide the service. The service providers sell the data they collect to other location data providers. Once the data is ingested, integrated, and shared in the broader ecosystem, there is no telling where it will go, who will be buying it, or what it will be used for.

In one use case, my team and I analyzed data from the top five location providers in the US and used the data to determine how many people visited approximately a thousand specific locations in the US. We could predict how many people would visit those locations and how long they would stay, and we could improve a business use case, even though we knew very little about those thousand locations.

2.2.2   *Do you like being tracked and monitored?*

Most people leave location services on all the time and are blissfully unencumbered by any worry about being tracked in each and every waking, and sleeping, moment, but they are still being tracked.

There are governments that use location data for nefarious purposes, and we will talk about those problematic situations, but for now governments are not our concern. In western democracies, the idea of some all-knowing Big Brother is a fiction, no matter what some politicians tell you. The real problem is commercial companies, specifically the younger, more intelligent, companies like Google, Amazon, Netflix,

---

[4] Technavio, "Top 10 Location Based Service Providers in 2017–21," *Technavio Blog*, May 10, 2017, https://blog .technavio.org/blog/top-10-location-based-service-providers-2017-21.

[5] "Google Maps Platform Coverage Details," *Google Maps Platform*, December 19, 2021, https://developers .google.com/maps/coverage.

[6] "Distance Matrix API," *Google Maps Platform*, December 19, 2021, https://developers.google.com/maps/ documentation/distance-matrix/overview.

and Airbnb. They are the most effective and intrusive users of data. These companies are problematic, but they are, for the most part, only concerned with making money.

As I noted earlier, Google could have built an innovative and novel business model, but they went with an advertising-based model: boring, dull, well understood, and surprisingly fragile. On the consumer-facing side of their business, and all the businesses listed previously, the goal is to get more people (viewers, users, eyeballs, etc.) to give more data, so they can sell more ads to the same people who provided the data in the first place.

On the other hand, Facebook has shown no regard for the social consequences of their platform, as long as their actions continue to boost engagement metrics on their platform. Not only does Facebook not care, but they actually work to increase these network effects. Facebook, and companies like them, are the reason the data ecosystem will change. They have taken the ability to hurt individuals, communities, regions, states, and nations to a new and frightening level. But while they are annoyingly circumspect in their mission and goals, Facebook is easy to deal with. Just don't use their platform. They are so nakedly aggressive in their unbridled use of data for unscrupulous purposes that the data ecosystem will be modified by competitors and governments, and not to Facebook's benefit.

The data ecosystem evolved unsupervised for the past hundred years. It has been a free-for-all, with companies taking data, storing it, and using it for nearly any purpose that they see fit. This is changing and will change rapidly over the next three to five years. Let's start to discuss what that future data ecosystem will look like.

2.3   The past is the past, but the future has not been written yet

Today, the world's most sophisticated companies are on the right path. They will determine how to collect, integrate, analyze, and use data on a global scale to target each individual that they are interested in. Data and analytics systems are getting better, faster, cheaper, larger, more accurate, and more specific each day, and they will only continue to get faster and more reliable.

However, as these systems, technologies, methodologies, and approaches improve, people should not allow their data to be part of this process in an unmanaged manner. It isn't beneficial to individuals for any company or governmental agency (foreign or domestic) to know where they are at all times. There is no legitimate need for them to record every place we visit.

The reason people allow it is that they do not consider the implications of being constantly tracked. In the next part of this chapter, we'll consider two real-world scenarios that make those implications crystal clear.

2.4   *On my way for the day . . . A Grand Day Out . . .*

As it has been explained in the Discipline and Punish: The Birth of the Prison by Foucault, being under surveillance can cause people to keep themselves from creating new ideas and causes the person to question himself and initiates a self-censorship movement in the society, which helps to create an adequate environment to rule the society easily by the oppressive regimes.[7]

—Emre Rençberoğlu

I'm out on a shopping trip with a mission of buying my wife a gift. My first stop is at Walgreen's to buy a Mountain Dew. My wife is monitoring my movements with a tracking app. No worries, I don't care that my wife, or the app, knows that I stopped at Walgreen's. She texts me and says, "Hey, I see that you are at Walgreen's on Central and Main. Did you pick up the toothpaste that I asked you to buy 4 times already?"

I have, indeed, forgotten the toothpaste again, this time because I was on a mission to find and buy the perfect gift for her. I walked right past the aisle and shelf and still have not purchased the toothpaste. I'm annoyed. I really do not like to forget things, and it is even more annoying that I have been reminded of my multiple instances of oversight.

Unfortunately, I have to text back that I have left the store and am on my way to my next stop. Should I go back to get the toothpaste, or should I carry on with my planned agenda? I decide to carry on, but I'll stop at the end of my journey to buy the toothpaste.

At the local mall I stop at a store I have visited multiple times over the past six months to look at the gift that I want to buy, but it is costly. My wife told me multiple times that we should dedicate our cash to other purposes, but I *really want* to buy this gift. Suddenly I realize that my wife is watching my movements. I leave the store without buying the gift and I am annoyed again. I should have turned off location services.

I head over to the electronics store for a gift for one of our children, and as I enter the store, my phone rings. It is my wife. She knows that I am at the electronics store and asks that I pick up a certain item at another store in the mall. This whole tracking situation has really put me off buying anything. We chat, and I go to the store to buy what she asked for. I go back to Walgreen's and pick up the toothpaste. I finish off my Mountain Dew and head home.

Now my mood has changed. Just the idea that someone is surveilling me, even if it is for a supportive purpose, is upsetting to me. You may brush this off as a foolish reaction, but this example demonstrates that surveillance of any kind has an effect on thoughts, behaviors, intentions, actions, and interactions, and perhaps not an effect we desire.

Give it a try. As a simple and easy thought experiment, take yourself through a day, any day. A day where you are free to do as you please, and give some thought to how you

---

[7] Emre Rençberoğlu, "Dark Side of Data: Privacy," *Towards Data Science,* Jan 27, 2020, https://towardsdata science.com/dark-side-of-data-privacy-ba2850de512.

would feel when someone you care about is watching your every move. Would you make different choices knowing that someone, multiple people, or companies are watching what you are doing? Would you spend money in a different manner? Would you go to different stores or locations? Would you take a different route? How would you change your actions and behaviors, given that your movements are being scrutinized?

2.4.1   *Your working day: Do you know who is watching you?*

Do you carry a company-issued mobile device? If so, not only does your family know where you are at all times, so does the company you work for. Now, at the very least, you have two people tracking your every move. Each time you go to the restroom, they know it. Each minute you spend in the cafeteria, they are aware of your location and the time you spend there. Your company may even know who you are having lunch with. Perhaps it is a colleague who just resigned. You may now be considered a flight risk. Did you recently get a call from the human resources department to touch base for seemingly no reason?

Let's discuss another work-related possibility. You have been assigned to a strategic project, and the team meets every Tuesday at 10 a.m. You have had a recent health problem, and one of the doctors that you need to see on a recurring basis is only available at the same time as the team meetings. Your manager has been alerted by the company's employee tracking system that you have missed recent meetings. The company's location services tracking system has located you in two different doctor's offices during the planned meetings.

Your manager sets up a meeting to find out about the project, not because it is time for an update or because your colleagues have missed you. The cause is that the surveillance system has flagged your movements as being out of the norm and needing to be investigated. How are you feeling, going into that meeting with your manager? Are you feeling happy and supported or are you feeling like you are under the microscope?

Almost every app you use on your device enables location tracking. In addition to all the people I mentioned, such as your family and employer, think about all the apps you use. Consider the intentions of those companies to understand you, your actions, the actions of your coworkers, and of your immediate and extended family.

We have not even started to discuss the use and integration of your data beyond location data. Now the fun begins. Let's discuss just a few of the data streams that all of us create on a daily basis.

2.4.2   *Browsing data: What are you looking at?*

Companies and organizations are looking at our browsing data so they can determine what information, content, and offers they can make to us. If they take the location data and add browsing data to it, they know where you went, the routes you took, and the time you spent at each location as well as the products you viewed, the content you read, the various options you considered. Did you view the same product on Amazon, the Wal-Mart site, and perhaps the Yeti site as well?

Each data source added to our profile exponentially increases the ability of companies to examine, analyze, predict, and target us with ever-increasing accuracy, and possibly manipulative messages and offers. If location data indicates where we are and have been, the combination of location data and browsing data not only identifies where we were and what we looked at, but now firms can infer much more about us, such as what we might be inclined to buy, or view, or recommend to our friends. The more data sources that are added to our profile and that companies have access to, the more those firms will know about us. It's an ever-increasing cycle of data compilation and targeting.

2.4.3 *Tangential interests vs. core interests*

We all browse information that is of tangential interest to us, but do the firms collecting information about us understand core interests versus tangential interests? In fact, those firms do not understand our varying levels of interest well at all.

Our daughter is a student at the University of Michigan, and she is interested in the Michigan football team. I am not very interested in American football or college football, but I enjoy talking about the Michigan football team with her, so I want to know who Michigan is playing, how the team did last week, what their overall record is, and any other high-level topical stories that are being discussed in any given week.

My location data indicates that I was recently in Ann Arbor, and my browsing data indicates that I looked at the final score of the Wolverine game with Maryland. From these data points, organizations could infer that I am a University of Michigan football fan. That would be partially correct, but it doesn't warrant the change in my information feed that I am seeing. I am seeing numerous stories about Michigan football, Big Ten football, Jim Harbaugh's ongoing complaint about Big Ten officiating, stories about the salacious off-field behavior of coaches and players, and other information related to college football. I am not interested in any of that.

This scenario illustrates the blunt targeting instrument that most companies are leveraging today. This scenario also illustrates why individuals have a perception and belief that data collection isn't that important. I hear people say things like, "Companies target me with offers and stories that I am not interested in. Therefore, they can't be doing much with my data, given how bad they are at understanding me and my true interests." What individuals are missing is that companies are not good at understanding the difference between tangential and core interests today, but they are getting better, and they will be much better at it in the future.

Companies of all types are getting better and better at collecting and using data to predict what we will do and what they want us to do. Just because companies are not good at targeting us today doesn't mean they will not improve over time. Collecting data of all types, and analyzing that data with ever-increasing accuracy and speed, is the goal of nearly all companies and will remain so for the foreseeable future. We cannot be complacent about their current lack of abilities. They will improve at achieving their goals, but will their aims and efforts align with ours?

2.4.4   *Infrequent or episodic transactions*

Most companies are not very good at understanding immediate needs, short-term needs, and the next actions of individuals.

Recently, my wife and I decided that we were going to buy a new car. We were investigating the Jeep line of automobiles. The Jeep Grand Cherokee was the front runner for a few months, but we did not have a chance to drive one. Both my wife and I were reading reviews and configuring cars online, and we agreed that this was the car for us. We visited three Jeep dealers in the Chicago area and, given the pandemic, the shortage of new vehicles was acute. Even so, no one from Jeep contacted us, and no one from the dealerships called us.

In the hopes that I might buy a Michigan football shirt or attend a college game with a total transaction value of $300, I was bombarded with Michigan and college football information. Considering that the type of car we were evaluating can cost as much as $80,000, I would have expected a similar level of targeting, but no. No one contacted us.

There are immediate windows of opportunity for browsing and location information. That data indicated that we were ready to engage with a company or companies to consider a significant purchase. We became interested and investigated options online and offline. We spoke to representatives of multiple companies, and we left a trail of online browsing and reading activity that was unmistakable, but no one followed up. If Jeep had been on its game, we might have purchased a car from them, but we pivoted in the middle of the process and changed our attention to electric cars.

We began to evaluate electric cars from GM, Ford, Audi, Tesla, and others. Our intensity of searching, browsing and physically visiting dealerships changed in a matter of days. These changes in behavior are easy to detect, but Jeep didn't pick up on the change. We were all over the Jeep website, reviews from third parties, and remarks from owners, and then we were gone. As soon as we appeared, we disappeared.

We drove a Ford Mustang Mach-e, talked about it, configured the car a number of ways, and then purchased a 2022 model.

So far in this chapter, you have seen that getting targeting right with only a couple of data streams is incredibly hard—the results to date have shown that to be so. We have talked about how consumers and individuals can get the mistaken impression that companies are not very well versed at collecting, storing, managing, and analyzing data, given the poor attempts at, and the results of, personalization, individualized offers, and messaging.

Let's continue to add data sources in order to understand the state of the art in using our data.

2.4.5   *Small repetitive transactions*

On the other end of the spectrum, there are companies that produce individualized offers, messages, and interactions with incredible accuracy and consistency. Netflix and Amazon are world class in using fast-moving data from small repetitive transactions for targeting. Think of what data you provide to Amazon.

If you are an Amazon Prime member, you may choose to purchase items from varying categories due to the free shipping on many items, sometimes delivered within an hour or at least on the same day. Possibly you like Amazon's simple return policy. No matter what your motivations are, Amazon has done an impressive job of giving us numerous reasons to consolidate our purchases on the Amazon platform.

In the process, you freely provide Amazon the following information:

- Credit card numbers, expiration dates, CVV codes, billing addresses
- Debit card numbers
- Bank account numbers
- Telephone numbers
- Several addresses:
  - Primary residence and secondary residence
  - Children at college
  - Mother, father, sister, brother, aunts, uncles
  - Friends, coworkers, and colleagues that you send purchases to
  - Your birthday and the birthdays of all the people that you send birthday gifts to
  - Religious affiliations (if not directly, then indirectly by the gifts, purchases, and timing of the items that you send)
- Your return preferences
- Grocery purchases and preferences via Whole Foods
- All of your interactions with Amazon, including transaction data, shipping data, and returns data
- Your notes to customer service: complaints, compliments (remember those?), requests for corrections and adjustments
- Stolen package reports

Amazon is great at personalizing what you see and what is offered to you because they know what you have purchased since you joined the site. Your entire purchase history and consumer profile is at the disposal of the Amazon data science, operations, marketing, affiliate marketing, pricing, and other Amazon teams to analyze your activity and behaviors.

Infrequent transaction cycles (such as car purchases) make it hard to analyze, create, and insert the optimal messages. But it is quite easy to personalize and deliver accurate fine-grained, targeted messages for purchases that happen on a regular cycle. The automation, frequency, and price paid for a single item can be used to infer a wide range of behavioral characteristics not only of a person, but of an entire household.

From the purchase of a 16-pack of Bounty paper towels every four weeks, Amazon can infer much. If the purchases are automated, they can infer that the purchaser is comfortable with technology and that they value having a clean house, convenience, and time. Perhaps they have a cleaning service, which would infer that they have disposable income. At a stretch, the purchase could infer that they do not care about climate change, since they are consuming so many paper towels. If Amazon can derive all these conclusions from your paper towel consumption habits and patterns, what could they make of all of your purchases as a whole?

2.4.6   *Data and the power of multiple data sources*

Analytics can be powerful, but the underlying data is the rocket fuel that powers the insights, targeting, messaging, and offers. When a company has a single source of data, such as location data, they can clean and organize the data to gain a clear picture of our locations and movements, and they can infer a number of characteristics of our actions and behaviors. However, as the number of data sources increases, the number of inferences and insights that they can create multiplies exponentially.

The most impressive firms and data science teams know and understand that the goal of all data collection efforts is to collect enough multifaceted data about a person, behavior, or situation to be able to analyze, model, predict, prescribe, simulate, and optimize their insights based on the interests of the parties executing the collecting and modeling activities.

Any and all companies collecting data are interested in you, your family, your friends, your colleagues, your coworkers, and even random people you may come across in a day. In the great majority of cases, their interests in you and your constellation of relationships are not aligned with your interests. Their interests, in a number of cases, will run completely counter to what you believe to be your best interests.

2.4.7   *Fresh or stale, just like bread*

To be of the utmost value, and to produce the most accurate results, data needs to be fresh. Not all data needs to be immediate, but all data needs to be relevant, and if it is recent it is much more valuable. Human behavior is dynamic and ever changing. The data collected, however, just needs to be complete and accurate enough that companies can rely on the data and models to hit the macro-objectives they are seeking to manage, like next quarter's revenue and profit targets.

In 2019 the COVID pandemic took the world by surprise and with great force. In January 2020 predictive models worked well and provided strategic information to a number of operational areas in businesses on a daily basis. In February 2020 there was a noticeable degradation in the models' results, but in March 2020 the models were off by a significant margin. The pandemic changed the world and how people were acting and operating.

Models are trained on data, and data comes from how people act and interact with systems, applications, organizations, and other people. Data collected, integrated, and cleaned appropriately provides an accurate representation of what people are doing and how they are behaving when the data is collected. If people continue to behave in a manner that is predominately the same as before, the data continues to be collected, and the models are run, producing predictions that are very accurate.

As human behavior changes and data is continually collected, the models are trained, retrained, and put into production. The subtle changes in behavior resulting from economic factors, the seasons, and holidays are accounted for, and the models continue to provide insights into what will be in the coming seconds, minutes, days, weeks, and months.

When there is an abrupt change in the world, and people change how they act in a dramatic manner, such as with the COVID pandemic, models do not continue to work as planned. Not only do they need to be retrained, but the models may also need to be recalibrated or rebuilt entirely.

Dramatic external change is not limited to external biological shocks. Dramatic external change can come from collective action. If we stop providing our data, models and data pipelines that rely on that data will not continue to work. You may think, as an individual, that your actions may not be enough, but that is not true. If we all take action and begin to contain and control our own data, we can take back control of what firms know about us and how they use our data.

The companies that are misusing and abusing our data rely on us to continue to provide them with data so they can keep making money. If we all act, those companies will have to change how they operate.

The takeaway from this section is that companies use our data to predict our actions for highly repetitive tasks, like engaging with social media, reading news from unedited and unconfirmed sources, buying a wide range of goods and services from platforms like Amazon, and using buy now and pay later sites like Klarna. For these sites to continue to leverage our data for positive and negative outcomes—positive and negative to us and the people we care about—we need to continue to provide them with our data. If we hold back our data, they cannot continue to predict, message, and engage with us in the same way.

2.4.8   *But day-old bread has its uses too*

Aggregating and accumulating data over time is exceedingly valuable. Organizations and analytics teams are not only interested in how to send messages right now; they are also interested in your long-term patterns of behavior, your travel patterns, your life stage, etc. Immediate, hot, or fresh data is imperative for sending a message about something you might be considering today, like where to have lunch or whether to buy that sweater, but an aggregation of data is best for understanding you and your preferences over time.

Let's look at a scenario to bring this to life. I grew up in rural Michigan. As an adolescent, it might have seemed that I would live in the small town I was born in for most if not all of my life. But a year after graduating from high school, my behavior changed. I moved out of my small town and began attending a small state college.

That is a substantial change, but not one that would predict with great certainty that I would stay on this new path. When I was working for a global technology company, we executed a project for a mid-sized college in the United States and found that first-generation college students were vulnerable to dropping out. It was obvious which students were at risk. Data related to class attendance, quiz and test scores, engagement with faculty, staff, and administration was considered. We worked with the college to design a data collection operation and an analytics program that produced lists of students who were at risk. We also developed and provided tailored analyses of each student's behaviors and suggested messages and actions that significantly reduced the dropout rate of the target population—first-generation college students.

Some data is more valuable for immediate analytics, personalization, targeting, and messaging, and other data is useful when it is aggregated and accumulated over time to understand longer-term trajectories and directions. After I graduated and moved to Chicago, no company, without collecting data over multiple decades, could know that I would move up the socioeconomic ladder, change jobs from an auto mechanic to a developer, live in a substantially different neighborhood, and begin a life that consumed different products, services, and more.

The bottom line is that your data has been, and can, and will be used for purposes that serve the companies that are executing the data collection and analytics projects and programs.

2.5　Whose interests are being served by leveraging your data?

The interests of the most aggressive and intelligent firms are to know you and your network of friends and family as well as, and in some cases better than, you do. The data they collect fuels their ability to gain an upper hand in their relationship with you. This ability to know you and your family and network of colleagues and friends does not come from analytics. Analytics play a role, but this capability comes from collecting, integrating, and using a wide range of data sources.

The goal of collecting these sources is to model every situation you and your network of individuals may encounter. The sources go beyond the facts customers provide freely to companies like Amazon. They include macro-economic factors from world governments: data related to property and personal crime, housing starts, unemployment, social assistance programs, food banks, charity operations, local sales and offers. With all this data, companies can model and predict millions of possible situations that you and the people you know and interact with will experience.

Once a modeled situation presents itself in your world, they will be ready to message you with an offer that is tailored to your immediate situation. But the offer is tuned to what the company wants and needs. Maybe they want you to buy more gifts, groceries, clothes, or cars, when you really need to reduce your debt. It's a case of striking when you are most vulnerable, rather than assisting when you are most in need. The point here is that they will be targeting you to maximize their plans and outcomes, not yours. It is not one really smart company executing this business plan. All top-tier companies are collecting, analyzing, and acting on data in this manner.

Compounding the problem, these companies are not only modeling and targeting each and every possible scenario that you and your network of people may encounter. They are also modeling every possible action and reaction of everyone they are interested in.

2.5.1   *This can only continue if we allow it*

Companies can only do this if we give them our data. Data is at the core of all of this modeling, acting, reacting, learning, amplifying, rescoping, targeting, messaging, and manipulating. Social media companies are the best in the world at data collection, analysis, and targeting, and their manipulation of people's attitudes and actions works on a massive scale. They actively work at cross purposes to the mental health and well-being of the world's citizens. You need to know that this is not how it needs to be, and we are not destined to continue on this path.

Scott McNeely said in 1999, "You have zero privacy anyway. Get over it."[8] He was right then, and to this day there is truth in what he said, but that doesn't mean this has to be the future for all of us. Many people, and maybe even the majority of people, will remain unaware of the use of their data and will continue to hand over their privacy and data, but not everyone has to act this way.

If firms can obtain, and continue to obtain, data in sufficient volume and variety, and with the right velocity, they can model and simulate the real world with enough specific detail that their actions can seem to be prescient. Their offers and actions can seem like they are perfectly timed with the right tone and tenor to entice us to take that offer even if it is not in our best or long-term interests, but that can only happen if we continue to, unwittingly, provide them with the free data to run their data and analytics operations and teams.

If we stop providing them with the data required, their engines will grind to a halt. Companies cannot produce analytical results without the data required to run the data pipelines, models, and operational engines.

You have the power to stop or significantly alter how this progresses. You can change the future. You can change how companies target you and your children. You can change it all. You just need to want to.

2.5.2   *Is it really possible to exit platforms?*

Recently, Lush, the personal care company, decided to take down many of its social media accounts. An executive of the company said, "he's 'happy to lose' $13 million quitting social media. 'We're talking about suicide, not whether someone should dye their hair blonde.'"[9] Whether people know it or not, social media companies, online platforms, and companies of all types can only exist and operate if we opt in and are complicit in their treatment of us. We do not have to participate. We should not participate. The state of play today is not the way it needs to be tomorrow.

So, yes, it is possible to exit platforms. You, your family members, companies, not-for-profit organizations, and all other individuals and firms have a choice. We can all leave any platform or service at any time.

---

[8] Scott McNeely, "You Have No Privacy—Get Over It," *Fox Business*, 1999, updated Mar. 4, 2016, https://www.foxbusiness.com/features/you-have-no-privacy-get-over-it.

[9] Felicia Hou, "Lush CEO says he's 'happy to lose' $13 million quitting social media. 'We're talking about suicide, not whether someone should dye their hair blonde'," *Fortune*, Dec. 1, 2021, https://fortune.com/2021/12/01/lush-quit-social-media-executive.

2.5.3   *Is it worth what you and we are paying?*

The "free" services being offered are not free to the company offering them. The "free" services that you and your family are using are not free to you. For-profit companies and not-for-profit organizations must pay their bills, cover their costs, and save money for a rainy day.

There is an observation and associated sayings that seem to have all originated from gambling and gaming (I first heard it in relation to playing poker): "If you look around the table and you cannot identify the person being taken advantage of, then it is you." One variation of the saying goes something like this: "If you are examining a business and you cannot identify the product or service, it is you."

The point is that the "free" services are not free. You are paying for them with your data and your agreement to allow these firms to observe, examine, aggregate, analyze, target, and sell you as a commodity. We have incrementally arrived at this position over the past 30 years by eroding our understanding about our data and its use, and we will incrementally move to a new position as well.

2.5.4   *Why is the online world different than the offline world?*

Let's use building a house as an example and compare that to what is happening in the online world. You hire a builder to build your house, and the builder provides you with a cost estimate for building it. The estimate includes all the material to build the house—all of those raw materials must be purchased from suppliers. Because no one has determined a good way to give you free materials, you must pay for them and the associated markup that the builder adds to those materials for his services including buying them, arranging for the materials to arrive at the site, and for the scrap to be removed from the site. When you pay for the house, you have to pay for all the materials, labor, permits, and inspections. This is normal and commonplace. Not paying for data is like the builder not paying for lumber or concrete. No supplier would provide the lumber or concrete for free so no houses would be built.

It is the same with your data. If these services do not have your data, they cannot exist, at least in the form they inhabit today—why should they be supplied with it for free? They should not; you should be paid for your data.

2.6   *Who are you aligned with?*

If you don't mind handing over your data freely and are unaware of how the data is created and used, you are aligned with and supporting the firms that are targeting you. If you are among the growing majority of people who feel otherwise, you are not.

You are not alone in this paradigm shift. The legislative framework is being put in place to support you in controlling your data. Let's look at why we would want to do this and how we can begin the process of doing so.

2.6.1   *What is in our best interests?*

You are currently giving your data to these online platforms, and they are packaging you like any other product and selling it to firms to target you on their online platforms. You are aligning with the people who are actively working to manipulate you. In what world is this in your best interest?

Best interests may be hard to see today, just as they were almost impossible to see five years ago when the European Union instituted the General Data Protection Regulation (GDPR).[10] Today the GDPR is the foundation for all data privacy protections that are being developed and adopted around the world. The nascent foundations of data empowerment are beginning today and will take root over the next few years. The EU has followed its groundbreaking regulation in the GDPR with a new data governance framework and proposal, the EU framework on data governance.[11]

It took five years for governments outside the EU to begin to formulate and enact legislation that follows the example of the GDPR, but that global movement is now underway. California's Consumer Privacy Act (CCPA) was passed in 2018.[12] More US states and national governments are considering following the EU and California's lead in drafting and enacting legislation in the areas of privacy and data protection.

A recent research report describes the current state of play:

> *This new digital economy is described in a variety of ways: as a cognitive capitalism, where a systematic process of privatization of information in different forms allows for maximization of profits (Bauwens et al., 2019; Fumagalli et al., 2019), as a data colonialism, in which data is used to subjugate and transform social relations (Couldry & Mejias, 2019), or as a form of surveillance capitalism, in which various technological apparatuses monitor humans and try to predict and control human behavior for the sake of profit (Zuboff, 2019). Regardless of the theoretical approach, the key assumption that current data mining practices are failing individuals and society remains at the heart of the problem.*[13]

The EU will continue down the path they started in 2016 with the drafting of the GDPR. The drafting of the EU legislation on data governance and the creation of a data commons or multiple data commons is complete. The work of enacting this legislation is underway. It is only a matter of time before this mode of operating becomes the standard in the EU and eventually around the globe.

As there was with the GDPR, there will be much hand wringing and many dire predictions from lobbyists, corporate executives, lawyers, US government officials, and many others who are really working on behalf of the corporations who benefit from monetizing our data, but their protestations will be futile. The movement has begun and cannot be stopped. Even if it is hard to see today, it will happen.

---

[10]GDPR.eu, "Complete guide to GDPR compliance," www.gdpr.eu.

[11]European Commission, "Proposal for a Regulation of the European Parliament and of the Council on European Data Governance (Data Governance Act)," *EUR-Lex*, Nov. 25, 2020, https://eur-lex.europa.eu/legal-content/EN/TXT/?uri=CELEX:52020PC0767.

[12]Wikipedia, "California Consumer Privacy Act," https://en.wikipedia.org/wiki/California_Consumer_Privacy_Act.

[13]Jan J. Zygmuntowski, Laura Zoboli, Paul F. Nemitz, "Embedding European values in data governance: a case for public data commons," *Internet Policy Review*, Sept. 30, 2020, https://policyreview.info/articles/analysis/embedding-european-values-data-governance-case-public-data-commons.

2.6.2 *Many paths to liberation: Beginning to control your data. Detoxing your data*

The first step is to turn off location services. Yes, you can do this on your mobile device. I have spoken with a number of people who didn't know you could do this. You can. This completely stops any person or company from tracking your location. This is a foolproof option for stopping all location tracking.

The problem is that when you want to use a map or to search for anything that involves a location, which is more common than you may think, you have to turn location services back on.

I was committed to the experiment, and I maintained my diligence for six months. My feed changed and I saw less information related to tangential interests, like the Michigan football example we discussed earlier in this chapter. I do believe that it made things better for me in that the number of what I consider irrelevant messages and offers was reduced during the experiment.

The second step is to delete unused apps. Examine all the apps that you use, and set their data sharing settings to the most restrictive options. This will enable you to keep your location services on and reduce the number of irrelevant messages and offers you receive.

2.7 Final thoughts

In this chapter we discussed what our role in the data ecosystem looks like today. We walked through an example of how we create data, where the data goes, and how that data is collected, stored, integrated, analyzed, and used and reused in ways that are counter to our basic values and interests.

We talked about how it may seem that companies are not very good at analyzing and targeting messages and offers to us in a number of common situations, and how in some of those situations, companies are not very adept in delivering the right messages at the optimum time. We also looked at where companies are very good at data collection, integration, targeting, and delivering compelling offers and messages. We then broke down the state of the art in leveraging data to understand human behavior by constructing and outlining a realistic scenario that involved location data and then built upon that data source by adding browsing and transaction data. This illustrates what the most sophisticated companies are doing today and what a majority of companies will do in the near future.

We brought the chapter to a close by identifying the existing and ongoing early-stage legislative efforts to create laws, structures, and operational environments that will help begin to change the balance of power relating to data.

As I noted throughout the chapter and will continue to discuss in the remainder of the book, our data belongs to us, not them. The economic value should accrue to us, not them. As I mentioned, not everyone, and not even a majority of people, will align with this view in the short term, but over the longer-term time horizon, this will become the predominant mode of operating when relating to data.

I am so very pleased that you will be in the group of people who are thought leaders and who will be in the vanguard of changing the way global citizens and societies view, use, monetize, and protect their data. You and your family and friends will live better lives for your being at the front of this unstoppable movement.

Summary

- We create the data that companies leverage to run their online services and apps.
- We need to be aware and knowledgeable about who we create data for, and what permissions and rights we sign away with little thought.
- Companies are constantly improving their ability to integrate numerous sources of data.
- Companies are using this integrated set of data to analyze, understand, and target individuals with messages and offers that may not align with their best interests.
- We can be more aware of our rights and control our data better.
- By controlling our data, we control which companies have access to us.
- This is the first step in our journey to control, protect, and monetize our data.

You and your data 3

Unequal knowledge about us produces unequal power over us.[1]

—Soshana Zuboff

Just look at the preceding list of topics. Data touches all of these aspects of life. All of us can benefit from being aware of the importance and impact of data on our daily lives. In addition to being pervasive in our lives, our relationship to data is about to change for the better. That relationship is about to change in ways that will make our data work for us.

---

[1] Soshana Zuboff, "You are now remotely controlled," New York Times, Jan. 24, 2020, https://www.nytimes.com/2020/01/24/opinion/sunday/surveillance-capitalism.html.

Attitudes toward and about data have changed and evolved over the past 60 years, just like many views, orientations, and norms in society. Just think about marijuana and gay marriage. In the past 20 years, these two topics went from being something that you should not talk about in polite company to being legal in most of the United States and in many countries around the world. Times, views, perspectives, and values change, and quickly in some cases. The prevailing societal views on data are about to change in ways that even most *experts* will not recognize.

3.1   *Origins of the internet and World Wide Web*

The internet came into being from the US military. "The precursor to the Internet was jumpstarted in the early days . . . of computing, in 1969 with the U.S. Defense Department's Advanced Research Projects Agency Network (ARPANET). ARPA-funded researchers developed many of the protocols used for Internet communication today."[2]

When the internet first began to grow outside the military and governmental domain, the early participants believed the internet could, would, and should be an egalitarian paradise where everyone had a voice and all people around the world shared freely without the intervention and motivation of money and personal gain.

One of the early participants in popularizing access to the internet was an intrepid entrepreneur, Barry Shein. "Barry Shein's The World STD was selling dial-up Internet on a legally questionable basis starting in late 1989 or early 1990, and then on an approved basis by 1992. He claims to be and is generally recognized as the first to ever think of selling dial-up Internet access for money."[3]

As the internet and the data generated by the increasing activity began to proliferate, a few people voiced concern about what could happen with the new streams of data. One of the early pioneers who outlined how the internet and data should be governed was John Perry Barlow, one of the founders of the Electronic Freedom Foundation (EFF; www.eff.org).

To this day, the US government, and most national governments, are struggling with how to legislate and regulate online behavior, commerce, and communications. In 1996, the US Congress was debating a law that was referred to as The Telecommunications Act of 1996.

> *Barlow and the EFF saw the law (a subsection of the larger law referred to as the Communications Decency Act of 1996) as a threat to the independence and sovereignty of cyberspace. Barlow argued that the cyberspace legal order should reflect the ethical deliberation of the community instead of the coercive power that characterized "real-space" governance. Since online "identities have no bodies", they found it inappropriate to obtain order in the cyberspace by physical coercion. Instead, ethics, enlightened self-interest and the commonwealth were the elements they believed to create a civilization of the Mind in Cyberspace.[4]*

---

[2] Kim Ann Zimmermann and Jesse Emspak, "Internet History Timeline: ARPANET to the World Wide Web," *Live Science*, June 27, 2017, https://www.livescience.com/20727-internet-history.html.

[3] "Commercialization of the Internet," *Wikipedia*, cited on Dec. 23, 2021, https://en.wikipedia.org/wiki/Commercialization_of_the_Internet.

[4] "John Perry Barlow," *Wikipedia*, cited on Dec. 22, 2021, https://en.wikipedia.org/wiki/John_Perry_Barlow.

Barlow's egalitarian ethos and aspirations for the better part of humanity to govern the workings of the internet and cyberspace are honorable, but development of the new online world did not go in the direction espoused by him and the EFF.

> *In 1989 [Tim] Berners-Lee drew up a proposal for creating a global hypertext document system that would make use of the Internet. His goal was to provide researchers [at CERN] with the ability to share their results, techniques, and practices without having to exchange e-mail constantly. Instead, researchers would place such information "online," where their peers could immediately retrieve it anytime, day or night.*[5]

Berners-Lee's development and code was the design and the foundation of the World Wide Web (WWW) and the invention of Hypertext Markup Language (HTML). With the advent of the World Wide Web and HTML, individuals and companies began to see the commercial and communication opportunities inherent in the first truly global platform.

Some would argue that radio and television are global platforms, due to their ubiquity and uniform distribution around the world, but their focus is local. Programming in and from the US is of limited interest to people around the world, as are selected programs from all countries. For example, American football is of little interest outside the US. Soccer is very popular all over the world, but the US population is, overall, uninterested.

The internet and the World Wide Web are the first properties and entities that are truly ubiquitous, uniformly distributed, locally accessible, widely available, translated into every language, and containing content of interest to all sections, segments, age ranges, and orientations of the human population.

When you want to know something, and you want to know it now, where do you go? On the internet. Everyone does. That is the way our lives work at this point in time, and it will be this way, in all likelihood, forever. The majority of data that is created is created on the internet, and most of the data is created with technologies and applications on the World Wide Web. These platforms are the basis for the vast majority of our interactions with other people and companies. This is where our data is being created and managed.

With unparalleled access to a growing and increasingly addictive global content repository come unprecedented levels of use and engagement, and the most interesting aspect for our discussion. The creation of data, more than the world has ever seen, is only getting faster, larger, and more widely distributed, and all our actions are actively complicit in that creation.

There is nothing wrong with the creation of data. It is just good to know that it is occurring with every click and tap that we execute.

---

[5] Michael Aaron Dennis, "Tim Berners-Lee," *Britannica*, updated Dec. 2, 2022, https://www.britannica.com/biography/Tim-Berners-Lee.

3.2   *Current views and attitudes toward data*

People in the general public are becoming more aware of the implications of the collection, use, and sharing of their data. A June 2021 study in the UK, "Information Rights Strategic Plan: Trust and Confidence," prepared for the Information Commissioner's Office (ICO), found that

> *There has been an indicative rise in the relative importance of the right to object to personal information being processed and a significant decline in the proportion claiming to have accessed their personal information.*
>
> *Although most have not exercised or experienced their rights, many are open to doing so in the future. However, for those who would consider exercising a right, most are unaware or not sure how to do this.[6]*

Governments have a role to play in making data collection and use more open and transparent. In the UK, the primary goal of the Information Rights Strategic Plan "is to increase the trust the public has in Government, public bodies and the private sector in terms of how personal information is used and made available."[7]

Healthcare data protection and sharing is a particularly sensitive topic. With the proliferation of wearable devices, such as Fitbit wristbands, Oura Rings, and Apple Watches, millions of people could be contributing a constant stream of biometric measurements on a real time basis. "But there's a problem: a significant public reluctance to allow healthcare services to share personal health data. [In the Information Rights Strategic Plan] it was found that only 47% of people would allow the UK's National Health Service (NHS) to pass on their data to public sector companies if it were used to improve the delivery of healthcare. The figure is 42% for private companies."[8]

In the UK, "levels of trust and confidence with different types of organisations are highest for the NHS and local GPs [general practitioners], and lowest for social media companies."[9]

The majority of the people who are aware of their data creation activities and who think about what is being done with their data are in the upper socioeconomic classes. Most of the people in the lower classes of economic prosperity don't give their data much thought at all.

---

[6] Mike Bamford and Michael Worledge, "Information Rights Strategic Plan: Trust and Confidence," Information Commissioner's Office (of the UK government), June 2021, https://ico.org.uk/media/about-the-ico/documents/2620165/ico-trust-and-confidence-report-290621.pdf.

[7] Ibid.

[8] Rich McEachran, "How to solve the healthcare data-sharing dilemma," *Raconteur*, Dec. 16, 2021, https://www.raconteur.net/healthcare/how-to-solve-the-healthcare-data-sharing-dilemma.

[9] Mike Bamford and Michael Worledge, "Information Rights Strategic Plan: Trust and Confidence," Information Commissioner's Office (of the UK government), June 2021,https://ico.org.uk/media/about-the-ico/documents/2620165/ico-trust-and-confidence-report-290621.pdf.

3.3   Some people don't have the luxury of thinking about data

Those who do not have the luxury of considering the implications of sharing their data are generally those who live in poverty or make just enough to get by. They are rarely in a position to worry about what is being done with their data.

3.3.1   People who live in poverty

There are billions of people living in poverty who do not think about their data. That is expected. When you are concerned about eating or safety, data is a far concern from your daily life.

"About 9.2% of the world, or 689 million people, live in extreme poverty on less than $1.90 a day, according to the World Bank. In the United States, 10.5% of the population—34 million people—live in poverty as of 2019"[10] (see figure 3.1). Furthermore, there has been the effect of the COVID pandemic. "The human cost of COVID-19 is immense, with hundreds of millions of people in the developing world reversing back into poverty. In 2020, between 88 million and 115 million people could fall back into extreme poverty as a result of the pandemic, with an additional increase of between 23 million and 35 million in 2021, potentially bringing the total number of new people living in extreme poverty to between 110 million and 150 million."[11]

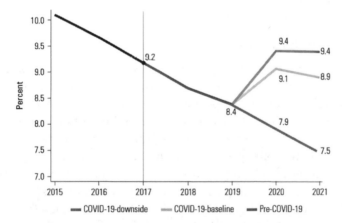

Source: Updated estimates based on Lakner et al. (2020), PovcalNet (online analysis tool), World Bank, Washington, DC, http://iresearch.worldbank.org/PovcalNet/, and Global Economic Prospects.
Note: Three growth scenarios are considered: (1) pre-COVID-19 uses the January 2020 *Global Economic Prospects* growth rate projections, predating the COVID-19 crisis; (2) COVID-19-downside and (3) COVID-19-baseline use the June 2020 *Global Economic Prospects* growth rates projecting a contraction in global growth for 2020 of 8 percent and 5 percent, respectively.

Figure 3.1   Nowcast of the global poverty rate at the US $1.90-a-day poverty line, 2015–21

[10]Andrea Peer, "Global poverty: Facts, FAQs, and how to help," *World Vision*, Aug. 23, 2021, https://www.world vision.org/sponsorship-news-stories/global-poverty-facts.

[11]World Bank, *Poverty and Shared Prosperity 2020: Reversals of Fortune*, 2020, doi: 10.1596/978-1-4648-1602-4, License: Creative Commons Attribution CC BY 3.0 IGO, p. xi, https://www.worldbank.org/en/publication/poverty-and-shared-prosperity-2020.

There may be a small percentage of this population who think about personal data, but we can estimate that this group of people will not be immediately interested in managing their personal data.

3.3.2   People who are living at subsistence levels

Living at the subsistence level is defined by Merriam-Webster's dictionary as "a level of income that provides only enough money for basic needs." The World Bank's *Poverty and Shared Prosperity 2020* report describes poverty as follows:

> *Poverty is a complex and multifaceted phenomenon. When poor people are asked in participatory studies what makes them feel poor, they indicate a wide range of deprivations: not having enough to eat, having inadequate housing material, being sick, having limited or no formal education, having no work, and living in unsafe neighborhoods.*[12]

> *About a quarter of the global population is living below the US $3.20 poverty line, and almost half is living below the US $5.50 line, compared with less than a 10th living below US $1.90. These figures translate to 1.8 billion people and 3.3 billion people at the US $3.20 and US $5.50 poverty lines, respectively.*[13]

If we take the people who are living in extreme poverty, approximately 850 million people, and we add the people who are living at or near subsistence levels, approximately 3+ billion people, globally 4 billion people have more immediate needs to tend to and are not concerned about their personal data.

3.3.3   Reducing poverty and why it matters

Data will continue to grow and be more important, so it will become important to this portion of the population as they and their children rise up out of poverty. Progress is being made in lessening the number of people in the world living in poverty, and these efforts will continue to bring billions of people into the portion of the population who *do* care. Given their previous and recent multifaceted deprivations, this population will not be keen to trade one type of disadvantage for another.

As these millions of people are making their way out of poverty and living on single digits of dollars of income per day, being paid a data dividend would make a meaningful contribution to their well being and ability to live a better life. This fact alone is worth changing how we think about data and how we work toward managing data for the benefit of each individual.

---

[12]Ibid., p. 43.
[13]Ibid., p. 39.

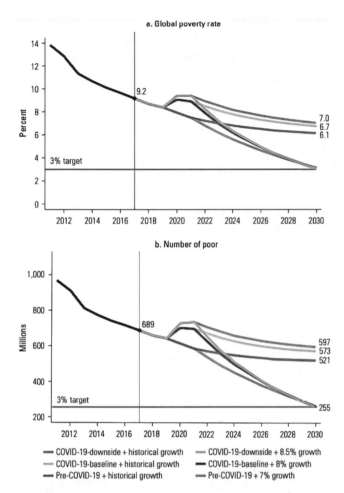

a. Global poverty rate

9.2

3% target

7.0
6.7
6.1

b. Number of poor

689

3% target

597
573
521

255

— COVID-19-downside + historical growth   — COVID-19-downside + 8.5% growth
— COVID-19-baseline + historical growth   — COVID-19-baseline + 8% growth
— Pre-COVID-19 + historical growth   — Pre-COVID-19 + 7% growth

Sources: Updated estimates of Lakner et al. 2020; PovcalNet (online analysis tool), World Bank, Washington, DC, http://iresearch.worldbank.org/PovcalNet/; World Bank 2020a, 2020b.
Note: All six scenarios use assumptions identical to those used in figure 1.4 until 2021. For 2021–30, scenarios with historical growth use the annualized growth rate for each country between 2008 and 2018. Another set of growth scenarios is chosen such that all economies grow at the same rate between 2021 and 2030, and such that the 2030 target of 3 percent extreme poverty is reached: these growth rates are estimated to be 7 percent for pre-COVID-19, 8 percent for COVID-19-baseline, and 8.5 percent for the COVID-19-downside.

Figure 3.2 Progress in reducing poverty: poverty rate and people

3.4   *How the general population thinks about data today*

A majority of Americans believe their online and offline activities are being tracked and monitored by companies and the government with some regularity. It is such a common condition of modern life that roughly six-in-ten U.S. adults say they do not think it is possible to go through daily life without having data collected about them by companies or the government.[14]

---

[14]Brooke Auxier, Lee Rainie, Monica Anderson, Andrew Perrin, Madhu Kumar, and Erica Turner, "Americans and Privacy: Concerned, Confused and Feeling Lack of Control Over Their Personal Information," *Pew Research Center*, Nov. 15, 2019, https://www.pewresearch.org/internet/2019/11/15/americans-and-privacy-concerned-confused-and-feeling-lack-of-control-over-their-personal-information/.

Chapter 2 talked about how people feel and act when they know or strongly feel that they are being monitored or watched as they go about their daily lives. This type of monitoring, actual or perceived, has a chilling effect on people's behaviors and mindsets. It causes the beginnings of paranoid feelings and leads to suspicion, skepticism, and cynicism.

Some of what we are seeing today in society comes from people believing that they are being watched and being fed false information and that facts are subjective. The Cambridge Analytica scandal was a turning point for many people around the world. For many people it was the first time they realized that their information was being bought and sold and used in ways that directly impacted them negatively.

Majority of Americans feel as if they have little control over data collected about them by companies and the government

% of U.S. adults who say ...

		Companies	The government
Lack of control	They have very little/no control over the data __ collect(s)	**81%**	**84%**
Risks outweigh benefits	They are very/somewhat concerned about how __ use(s) the data collected	**81%**	**66%**
Concern over data use	They are very/somewhat concerned about how __ use(s) the data collected	**79%**	**64%**
Lack of understanding about data use	They have very little/no understanding about what __ do/does with the data collected	**59%**	**78%**

Note: Those who did not give an answer or who gave other responses are not shown.
Source: Survey conducted June 3-17, 2019.
"Americans and Privacy: Concerned, Confused and Feeling Lack of Control Over Their Personal Information"

PEW RESEARCH CENTER

Figure 3.3   American views and attitudes about data collection

People generally do not like to be subject to coercion, monitoring, manipulation, or clandestine surveillance. There is no evidence that there is an overarching coordinated effort to monitor the general population, as predicted by George Orwell. But there are many organizations that would like to have more accurate, recent data to improve products, services, pricing, profitability, research, insights, ideas, and plans for the future.

We are at a point where data collection is imperative for a wide range of organizations to function optimally and continually improve, but it is time to redefine how we think about our data and if we *want* these organizations to have access to our data and on what terms. Before we can think about redefining how we think, each of us should first understand how we think about data right now.

3.5   *How do you think about data today?*

Given that you are reading this book, we will assume that you are aware, interested, and care about data in general.

For clarity, I have spoken with people who are

- Aware, interested, and care, but resigned to the view that nothing can be done to change how data is created and managed.
- Aware and interested and simply do not care. These people feel that the existing arrangement is fine. Companies can have all their data for free search, email, and other services.

Then there are people who are unaware, disinterested and do not care.

People will move back and forth along that spectrum. My goal is to move people on the margin toward being more aware, interested, caring, and actively engaged in understanding and acting on topics related to their data.

The vast majority of us grew up in an environment where data was not important economically, socially, or individually. It was reasonably common knowledge, or at least not a secret, that companies like grocery store chains, insurance companies, and others gave data away or sold data for small amounts of money and put few to no restrictions on the subsequent uses of that data.

Data was given away, not talked about, not governed, or protected, and not examined in detail by most of society, and this is still true for the most part. No one gains this knowledge or appreciation by intuition or is naturally born with it. Knowledge about data needs to be taught, like any other subject, but data is a relatively new subject, and it has a completely new context and meaning, and a multitude of new uses in today's world. Do you think that the companies who collect, store, and use your data, own or co-own your data? Companies would like you to think that they do own your data and that you are lucky to have access to it. The reality is just the opposite.

As we have discussed, it is a fluke of history that data is treated in this manner. Data is only treated this way due to a widespread lack of understanding of its ownership and a total lack of appreciation of the potential of data monetization for each individual and every company.

The majority of companies would like the current view to remain the prevailing view in the minds of the majority of people, and it probably will remain so for a few more years, but as we have discussed, times are changing. Views are changing, laws are changing, people are rising up out of poverty, and data is at the heart of many of these changes.

Companies do not own your data, you do. Companies do not co-own your data, you own it alone, and as a single owner you have all the rights and privileges that come with ownership. Most people do not understand the concept of licensing, even though they sign up for licensing agreements on a regular basis—almost daily . In fact, the companies are the licensees in the data world. You are the owner.

This relationship only seems reversed due to the accidental nature and history of data, the intentions and overtly duplicitous acts of companies, and the lack of laws and governmental regulations to enforce the natural ownership/licensing relationship in relation to data. When we bring these factors together, we have the upside-down market and environment that we see on a global basis.

> **Defining "ownership" and "licensing"**
>
> *Ownership*: This is where you own the rights to something, such as a car, a house, an album, or a book. You can do what you want with these items because you have purchased them or were granted ownership rights by a previous owner. You own the item. It is yours. You can modify it, sell it, destroy it, donate it, or gift the rights to another person.
>
> *Licensing*: You don't own these items. You have limited rights to use them under certain circumstances. Examples are a copy of a software program, like Microsoft's Word, access to and use of the search function from Google, or a car that you have leased. You don't own any of these things. You have licensed them from Microsoft, Google, a car manufacturer, or another party in the automotive supply chain. The companies that own these items grant you a limited use license as long as you live up to the terms of the agreement. All you can do is use the service or asset; you cannot sell, modify, or otherwise change the asset or service.

Once the legal framework for data ownership is in place, this upside-down situation will be reversed, and you will be the overt and clear owner of your data—all your data.

3.5.1 You own your data

Companies shouldn't be able to tell you what they will do, might do, and could do with something you own. That is like Ford telling you when and how you can drive your car. You would not buy a car from a company that claimed ownership rights over how you could use a car even after you bought the car. Would that make sense?

Since you *own* your data, you have the full rights and abilities to grant or revoke a limited use *license* for your data. For example, let's say that you don't like how a company uses your data to target messages to you. You will be able, in the future, to revoke their right to use your data. That is the first step that GDPR has taken in relation to data owned by EU citizens.

Perhaps you don't like how a platform, any platform—Amazon, Netflix, Google, WeChat—uses your data. Maybe they sell your data to a company that produces products you don't like or that you believe are harmful to the Earth or a portion of the population. Rather than revoking the outright use of your data, in the future you will be able to assign a monetary value to each data element or class of data elements (e.g., transactional data, browsing data, biometric data, demographic data), and the companies who want to use your data will have to pay you.

   In the near future, you will proactively be able to manage, restrict or revoke access to, delete, and modify erroneous data, because you are the owner of the data. Companies who want to leverage and use your data free of charge and with very few restrictions will have to abide by the rules you set for your data and pay the rates that you demand for specific uses of defined data types. The current legislation in the EU (outlined and described in chapter 4) will create a data commons environment where data will be collected, stored, and managed. As part of that data commons, you can manage the access to your data and set the price for using your data. In effect, you will be able to create and enforce your ownership rights to your data.

Data ownership and data monetization—an example

What if you don't like how airline companies are contributing to climate change? You set the price for any airline to access and use your data in their operations, marketing, and analytics efforts at 100 times, or 1,000 times, or a million times the price that you would charge a company that is involved in organic and sustainable farming. Or perhaps you want the organic farmers or organic industry as a whole to have complete and free access to all your data, because you believe in their inherent value and contribution to the Earth and society at large.

This is where we are heading, this is the future. You will be recognized by law and by governments as the sole and rightful owner of your data, and you can, as part of your ownership rights, enable or revoke access to your data, set the price and terms of use for any element of your data or all of your data, correct any erroneous data, and delete your data.

For example, you might be happy for Amazon to have access to your purchase history because they give you a free Prime membership when you do so. You are happy with these terms and therefore provide Amazon a revocable right to analyze your transactional data that originated on their platform. But perhaps, at the same time, you want no commercial companies to have access to your current or historical health records: the diagnoses provided by your doctors, and the prescriptions that have been prescribed and filled.

   You may not be aware that it is available, but I was reviewing health care prescribing data today. Are you happy that any data and analytics professional can buy and access your health care data at any time? At least in the US, your health care data is all for sale today, and you have no say in the matter, but in the future you will. Change is coming in the area of data ownership and the ability for each person to benefit from their data.

3.5.2   *Think about how your data is being treated*

We all need to start thinking about our data: Begin to be aware of the current state of access and use in relation to your data. Think about the data you create. Think about who has access to your data today. Can you trust them to do what is best for you and your family? Do they want the same things that you do? Are they and their team of data scientists working in harmony with your view of a better future?

Be aware of the good things that are happening with regards to data. Support these efforts. Be vocal about owning your data. While it is difficult for you to manage your data today, there will be foundational changes coming, and you will benefit from those changes.

3.5.3 *Think about your children*

As a parent, it is your duty and your responsibility to speak to your children about their data and how they are continuously creating data. Let's start with the parenting of small children—babies, toddlers, and children at very young ages.

ELECTRONIC DISTRACTION

We all see it: parents handing their children electronic devices in restaurants, parents pushing strollers down the street with the children in a reclining position affixed to a screen, children sitting in their car seats watching a screen.

Children are being given electronic devices to distract them at younger and younger ages. These children are creating data, and that data is being used to create new interfaces, new games, new modes of engagement, all of which are highly addictive. Companies are working to build games and interfaces that cater to and engage younger and younger children. This is a problem. Most parents would not give a toddler a cigarette, but they will, and do, give them internet-connected devices to keep them quiet. Both are addictive, and one is currently accepted by society, the other is not.

These toddlers are creating data that is being used to analyze, understand, and target them. Seems a bit unfair, but that is the world we live in today.

TEACHING RESPONSIBILITY

As our children grew up, my wife and I watched and monitored their activities. We limited their screen time, game time, and time where they were connected to the internet. One tactic we used was that their computers were in a common area and could not be moved. Mobile phones were not very capable or engaging back then, so we didn't have to deal with the portability issue. When they were old enough to understand the conversation (I believe they were 4 and 7 years old), we started to talk about their games, online browsing and viewing, and potential interactions with online platforms.

They both played a game where they had a house, their own avatars, simulated friends, and community members. This was a single player game, so they did not congregate with real friends in an online environment—that would come later. We asked how much the game cost. They responded that it was free. We explained that it did not cost them money to play the game, but that the game was not free. They asked what we meant. We went on to explain that they gave their name, age, email address, location, and player activity to the company in order to play the game.

The game had activities like fishing or making things that could be bartered for upgrades (such as a better fishing pole) or furniture or food. This game feature was useful, since we could use the game play as an example of non-monetary economic exchanges. This was a new form of value exchange, but one that they understood easily and immediately.

We explained that as they played, their data was the price they paid to play. They commented that providing their name and address was not a high price. We explained that the game play also generated data. We went on to explain that by watching how quickly they fished and made craft items, and how much they saved before they engaged in bartering and what they bartered for, the game company could see their engagement, their orientation to saving, the price that was optimal for the upgrades and food. We explained that the game play provided a great deal of insight into their psychology and economic orientation, which enabled the game company to change the game to keep them playing for longer and longer sessions, which we noticed and pointed out to them. This game was a turning point for them.

BEING INFORMED

For the past two decades, our family has been talking about the intrinsic and extrinsic value of data, the tradeoffs between paying with money or paying with data, why we see the messages and advertisements and offers that we do, and what we can do to protect our data, our identities, and our well-being by being smart about when, how, where, and how much data we provide to any and all companies, academic institutions, and government agencies.

Over and over as our two children came back to the dinner table, we discussed the motivations for companies to provide "free" games, platforms, software, and devices. They have grown into very savvy data producers and consumers. They are now in their twenties.

All of our choices to provide data are simple choices. We need to be aware that we are making conscious choices. This is not a warning to not go on the internet, and I am not suggesting that children should not ever be given games or allowed to participate in social networks or browse the internet. Our adult children do all of those things, but they are aware of the data ecosystem that is active and in play at all times.

As a recent example, when we were setting up our Disney+ streaming service, we created profiles for all four of us. As we sat in our living room, I believe it was our daughter who spoke up and asked if we really wanted to have four profiles, since that would provide more data on our viewing habits to Disney. We discussed it and agreed that it would be interesting to see if Disney did a better job of providing entertainment suggestions based on the viewing history of each of the users in our household. It was very satisfying to see our children actively questioning a choice in real time and understanding the ramifications of that choice on the data that we would be and have been generating.

We taught our children to think about their choices critically and proactively. That is all a parent can do. We should all be doing this with every child that we are responsible and accountable for.

3.5.4 *Worldwide data creation*

It is a rather daunting task to think about all 7.9 billion people in the world. "As of January 2021 there were 4.66 billion active internet users worldwide, ~59% of the global population. Of this total, 92.6% (4.32 billion) accessed the internet via mobile devices."[15]

To be frank, I don't, on a regular basis, sit down to think about all the people in the world and their data. It is an immense amount of data. "There are 2.5 quintillion bytes of data created each day at our current pace, but that pace is only accelerating with the growth of the Internet of Things (IoT). Over the last two years alone 90% of the data in the world was generated."[16]

When people do think about it in aggregate, on a global scale, they often say the subject area is too large to contemplate. Maybe they are right, but we as humans generally don't act on a global scale; we start with ourselves, our community, our nation, and maybe our global region. Good ideas take hold and spread around the world. We don't have to change the world by our actions alone, but our actions do help to reinforce and spread good ideas. We don't have to do it all ourselves, but we have an ability to do our part.

Don't let the scale of the issue intimidate or immobilize you. Change is coming, and you can play your part of this global movement.

3.5.5   *Thinking about how to manage your data*

You probably don't think about managing your data across all the platforms and systems that you engage with on a daily or regular basis. As we live and operate today, doing so would take up a significant amount of your time and is currently a completely unrealistic expectation.

As laws change, and data commons are created, interfaces for data management are created and made available to the public, data exchanges are created and come into operation, and data monetization levels, norms, and fees are created, more people will begin to access and manage their data. Managing and monetizing your data is not possible today, but it will be in the coming years. Just as you now order food from a local restaurant via a delivery service, or buy a car, or pay your bills via the online presence of your bank or service provider, you will go online and manage your data to calculate and deliver the data dividend that you have budgeted as part of your monthly income.

Most people in the world do not have streams of passive income. "Passive income includes regular earnings from a source other than an employer or contractor. The Internal Revenue Service (IRS) says passive income can come from two sources: rental property or a business in which one does not actively participate, such as being paid book royalties or stock dividends."[17] A data dividend is another form of passive income.

---

[15]Joseph Johnson, "Worldwide digital population as of January 2021," Sept. 10, 2021, https://www.statista.com.

[16]Bernard Marr, "How Much Data Do We Create Every Day? The Mind-Blowing Stats Everyone Should Read," *Forbes*, May 21, 2018, https://www.forbes.com/sites/bernardmarr/2018/05/21/how-much-data-do-we-create every-day-the-mind-blowing-stats-everyone-should-read/.

[17]James Royal, "20 passive income ideas to help you make money in 2022," *Bankrate*, Sept. 19, 2022, https://www.bankrate.com/investing/passive-income-ideas/.

Think about how nice that will be. Money for doing the things that you were going to do anyway, and a stream of money that keeps coming each new week, month, or year.

3.5.6 *Reaping a monetary reward from companies using your data*

Passive income is a new concept for the majority of people. Data monetization stems from the concept of the ownership of data being held by the individuals who created and are creating the data. Given that you as an individual own the data, and you are providing a limited license to commercial, not-for-profit, and governmental organizations to use your data on the terms and conditions you set, you will be the person who reaps the financial benefit from those organizations leveraging and using your data.

The laws that are being drafted now envision that each person will be able to access the entire universe of their data and be able to set usage conditions and rules, monetary terms for each data element, date ranges for where data can be used and where it cannot be used, exclusion lists of companies that cannot use your data, and inclusion lists of preferred companies that can use your data as you have designated on preferred terms.

You create data daily and you get to use Facebook and Google search and free email for your data. "Google earned $147 billion in revenue from advertising in 2020, or 80 percent of its total, while Facebook earned $84 billion in revenue from advertising, or 98 percent of its total."[18] Who do you think is getting a better deal today from using your data: Google and Facebook, or you?

You won't be paid billions of dollars, but you will be paid. This corrects a market imbalance and ownership issue that has gone on for far too long—over 100 years. You should be getting paid for the data you create on a regular and ongoing basis, not the management teams of some random companies.

3.5.7 *Carrot and stick*

Think of the companies and causes that you want to support. Now think of the companies that you do not agree with and the damage they do to the Earth, to society, and to people. What drives all of these companies? Money and the acquisition of money. What better way to support or deter these companies than providing them with more money or taking money away from them?

Sure, it feels good to post a scathing remark on social media, but do you think that the CEO of the company really cares? Believe me, I worked with a number of them, and they don't care about your posts. What they do care about is corporate performance and growth, typically denominated in monetary terms. Yes, they all talk about products and services and helping the world, but it really comes down to the performance metrics around revenue.

---

[18]"Washington Post - Schar School tech poll," *Washington Post*, updated on December 22, 2201, http://mng.bz/41Qa.

The data you create is yours, and the revenue stream from that data should be yours. Currently, you give your data for free without limitations, and companies provide you with email, search, and other services. As I have said, it's not a fair trade or exchange, but let's think about it in a slightly different light. When you go to the grocery store or gas station, will they let you trade them your access to email or search function for a day, a week, or a month for a loaf of bread or gasoline? No, they won't, and it is a ridiculous idea for a barter transaction, partially due to the fact that it is impossible to execute. But if you go to either of those businesses with cash from your data dividend, they will be happy to sell you products and services.

When you hear about fines that are levied for non-compliance, they sound impressive, and it appears that those fines might be enough to change their practices, operations, and behavior, until you compare the fines to the revenue of the companies. The fines are nothing and have no deterrence impact on these companies.

Enrique Dans, a Senior Advisor for Innovation and Digital Transformation at IE University, Madrid, recently wrote about how far technology companies will go to avoid complying with GDPR:

> The French privacy authorities (CNIL) are fining Google €150 million and Facebook €60 million for intentionally making it difficult for users to opt out of the installation of cookies on their computers, a breach of the country's law.
>
> According to French privacy laws, opting out of cookies on any online service has to be as simple a procedure as accepting them. . . .
>
> This [practice is referred to] as dark patterns; designing user interfaces to encourage or discourage certain behaviors, in this case, to try to prevent people from refusing to install cookies, making it more difficult to monitor and track their activity and, therefore, losing value as an advertising target.
>
> These companies prefer to face possible fines rather than give up information on all the users who try to consult their pages without being logged in. In a bid to force Google and Facebook to stop their shenanigans, the French regulator, which says it has received numerous complaints from users, says if the companies haven't fixed the problem within three months, they will face fines of up to €100,000 per day.
>
> In December 2020, the French regulator fined Google and Amazon €150 million and €35 million respectively for the same type of violations. Google was fined a further €50 million for GDPR violations.
>
> This is not being anti-American: this is just Europe demanding all companies to comply with its rules. We are seeing a growing global regulatory offensive to rein in Big Tech, and which clearly marks a change of era. We will see how far the regulators are able to go and how this impacts users.[19]

Fines are good for filling the coffers of governmental agencies, and we should clearly keep fining technology and media companies on a daily basis.

---

[19]Enrique Dans, "Will this be the year the regulators really crack down on Big Tech's abuses?" *Medium*, Jan. 8, 2022, https://medium.com/enrique-dans/will-this-be-the-year-the-regulators-really-crack-down-on-big-techs-abuses-9bfe74564b0d.

It is clear that the only way technology and media companies continue to operate as they do is if we continue to let them have and use our data for free. Those companies want your data and do not want the world to change as it relates to data. But it is too late for that, and they know it. That is one of the reasons why these firms have hired so many lawyers and lobbyists, to fight change.

I have just spent a significant amount of time and energy outlining and describing many of the pertinent aspects of your relationship with your data. I hope that you are feeling more informed and empowered when considering what actions you can take in relation to controlling, protecting, and ultimately, monetizing your data.

Let's now move on to a discussion of what is changing in the data ecosystem that will facilitate your new relationship with your data.

3.6 Green shoots and new beginnings

As we have been discussing, data is a unique resource. We talked about all the "data is the new X" statements in chapter 1. Data is the new sun, the new oil, even the new bacon. The comparisons of data to a wide range of commodities continues, and I am sure that you can find many more comparisons if you search them out.

According to Doug Laney, former Gartner analyst, global thought leader, best-selling author, and Innovation Fellow, Data & Analytics Strategy, at West Monroe, data or information has the following unique characteristics:

- Is non-rivalrous
- Is non-depleting
- Is regenerative and nearly unlimited
- Has relatively low inventory costs and transportation/transmission costs
- Is more difficult to control and own
- Is ecofriendly
- If you spill it, you can't clean it up[20]

Data is truly and radically different than other commodities that the world has known in the past, and it should be treated in new and substantially different ways. Thought leaders around the world are working on innovations at the national level to change how societies, governments, individuals, and companies govern, store, manage, use, protect, and pay for data.

In the UK, Tim Berners-Lee and Nigel Shadbolt were appointed as information advisors to the government in June 2009. The duo led the team that developed the site data.gov.uk. The animating idea behind their efforts, including data.gov.uk, is to enable and drive "The opening of more data sources [to] super-charge the public sector of the future and drive innovation, says Shadbolt."[21]

---

[20]Doug Laney, "Information is not the new Oil," Tweet, cited on Jan. 15, 2022, http://mng.bz/Q8aw.

[21]Oliver Pickup, "Web creator Tim Berners-Lee on the future of data," *Raconteur*, Dec. 6, 2021, https://www.raconteur.net/technology/tim-berners-lee-future-data/.

Also, Shadbolt is the chair of the Open Data Institute:

The chair of the Open Data Institute (ODI)—who's been principal of Jesus College at Oxford University since 2015, among other roles—points to the success of open data pioneer Transport for London (TfL). Often held up as an exemplar of open data, TfL offers data feeds and guidelines about air quality, cycling, walking, planning and more. In 2017, Deloitte calculated that TfL's release of open data generated annual economic benefits and savings of up to £130 million for travelers, the capital, and the organization itself. Additionally, many private businesses have taken advantage and cashed in on the open application programming interfaces (APIs).[22]

"We are starting to gain a sense of what data's going to make a difference—everything from emissions to insulation. There's a whole network of interconnected data types that we can bring together, much of it held in the public sector, and some of it held in the private sector," Shadbolt says. "We need to begin that work on joint public-private enterprises, though we are beginning to see the private sector, with its commitments to ESG, saying 'we now have to have a public purpose as well as a private one.'" Publishing some of this data "would be a great first step", he adds.[23]

When the pair founded the not-for-profit ODI nine years ago, the mission was to "connect, equip and inspire people around the world to innovate with data". For public sector technology to thrive, however, public trust is critical, says Berners-Lee, who notes a difference in attitudes to tech in the UK compared to the US. "Typically, in the UK people trust the government and don't trust [the tech] industry, and in the US people trust industry and don't trust the government," he says. More should be done to assuage fears about how tech giants handle user data, he adds. "To an extent, it's how people are brought up and therefore cultural. But for people in the UK to trust these large American companies then you need to have serious legislation and regulation."[24]

3.7   Final thoughts

The data landscape of the past is nothing like what the data landscape of the future will become. The current hodgepodge of efforts underway around the world may not seem like a unified movement, and they are not, not yet, but those efforts are moving in the same direction, and that tide will gain momentum and force in the coming weeks, months, and years.

There is no putting the genie back in the bottle. No matter what anyone says, data will be governed and treated differently in the coming years. The economic, social, monetary, and societal value of data will be more evenly distributed across societies, groups, and individuals.

Understand, know, and become a part of this movement. Talk about it at social gatherings. Post on social media. Talk with your professional colleagues who are involved in the life cycle of any and all data. Reach out to your elected government officials, and tell them that legislation related to data and your rights needs to be a priority, because it is

---

[22]Ibid.
[23]Ibid.
[24]Ibid.

for you, and it needs to be a priority for them. Spend time teaching your children about the movement so they can be critical thinkers and make informed decisions about their awareness, engagement, and level of care they actively put forth relating to their data.

Social media does a significant amount of damage to the world by algorithmically targeting people in the developing world with messages of division. Those people would benefit the most from a data dividend. Even if you don't need the money and see it as a marginal addition to your income, think of the double benefit to the developing world. Less hurtful propaganda will be spewed at people from their mobile devices and computer screens as money flows into their households. That alone is worth helping the nascent movements around the globe to come to fruition.

Summary

- It is ironic that the internet was a spin-off of a US military project that was extended by a European research and academic institution that was shaped by libertarians and free thinkers. What a combination of parents!
- The invention of the internet and World Wide Web has changed the landscape of data forever.
- Data is portable, mobile, fast moving, and can be used in a plethora of ways, none of which diminish past or future uses.
- We need to realize that we are the owners of our data.
- We need to ask ourselves how we can protect, manage, and monetize our data.
- Our data should be used primarily for our benefit.
- Control of our data is coming soon, and we need to start thinking about how to make the most of that control now.

Trust

4

This chapter covers

- Current efforts to slow or stop the evolution and expansion of proactive access, management, and monetization of data by individuals
- The state of trust in companies in general, and trust in technology and media companies in particular
- The value of data to you, and the introduction of the data dividend
- Change driven by law through the governments of the EU, Australia, US, and the relevant US states

The original idea of the web was that it should be a collaborative space where you can communicate through sharing information.[1]

—Tim Berners-Lee

---

[1] Tom Herbert and Alice Budd, "Sir Tim Berners-Lee: Net worth, best quotes and incredible achievements of the World Wide Web inventor," *Evening Standard*, March 13, 2019, http://mng.bz/MlQ7.

Historically, the general population in many societies believed that large organizations, governments, and leaders were able to set a long-term course of sustained improvement for us as individuals, societies, and perhaps for all of mankind; able though not necessarily willing. Even though they may have doubts, people can and do rely on those entities to chart long-term and beneficial visions and missions for our collective future.

Corporations have a vested interest in making the user base believe they can rely on the corporations to improve the quality and safety of society. They create campaigns describing how they collect, create, store, manage, integrate, and leverage data. The messaging sounds either positive, innocuous, or safe, but it's more often confusing. One of the goals of these programs is to slow or stop change that enables individuals to access, manage, and monetize their data. These lobbying efforts and associated proposals are very well designed, funded, and planned, and they are being executed in an orchestrated manner that is designed to counter improving our access to data.

When it comes to our data, these organizations lack the will to produce a data paradigm that will effectively protect personal data, because it runs counter to their own financial interests. Effecting change will require a movement outside of corporate interests. The movement needs our voices, our insights, our vision to define and refine it and make it a reality. But to help this movement, we need to know about the global environment that surrounds the perceptions, beliefs, and trust related to the handling of our data.

Trust is foundational in all human endeavors. This new data ecosystem needs to engender trust through new and existing organizations, to function efficiently, effectively, and in the best interests of all parties. We need new frameworks governing the data ecosystem, like data unions, to manage and monetize our data.

In this chapter we will discuss the world as we find it today. We will examine local, state, national, and international initiatives, laws, and pending and proposed legislation; research at think tanks, institutes, non-governmental organizations; positions, and actions from for-profit companies; and more. We will examine views, motivations, mindsets, orientations, proposals, and concepts related to our data.

First, there are headwinds pushing against improving our individual ability to access, manage, and monetize our data.

4.1   Forces that are working against our best interests

There is opposition to change in the world of data from entities that profit from today's data ecosystem. Let's examine their primary approaches to and reasons for opposing progress in relation to data.

First, several companies are sponsoring operations to convince legislators to maintain the status quo. They want more leeway to exploit data and keep all the benefits for themselves, commensurate with their near monopolistic position to leverage and influence data.

Second, there are funded and planned initiatives that are simply bad ideas that take time, money, and resources away from where real efforts need to be focused to drive effective change. They shroud the initiatives in messaging about being helpful and concerned with how data is used, even while they know they will fail, encouraging the status quo.

Third, many organizations know that they can use the desire to give individuals access and power over their data to give those same companies more power over data. They assume people prefer freedom from choice.

In spite of these corporate motivations to keep things as they are, change is coming. Even so, we must be diligent and not take change for granted. Now that you are aware of these efforts, you can be attuned to developments that sound interesting and positive at first glance but really are meant to slow down, forestall, or stop the evolution of our relationship with our data.

In the next section, we will examine the external world as it is today in relation to how our data is created, protected (or not), and used. Several very promising approaches, plans, frameworks, and laws have been developed or are underway. These are truly the actions and initiatives that will make life better for future generations. It is beneficial for us to be aware of these actions, initiatives, and laws.

4.2   Trust

Trust is a crucial element in our world. It can be gained, lost, and regained to some extent with significant effort. The lack of trust, however, is a real and widespread problem everywhere.

Media companies and organizations tend to package opinion alongside news in such a way as to make them indistinguishable from each other, fueling the distribution of misinformation and disinformation. This realization hit home to me in 2008.

4.2.1   *Infotainment is not news, and alternative facts do not exist*

I was on a work-related trip with a young employee who had traveled from another country to accompany me at a business meeting with a major telecommunications carrier. It was an important meeting with a new client and a crucial milestone for this young employee to present our product roadmap.

When she arrived at breakfast, I asked if she was rested and ready for the meeting. She replied that she did not get much sleep. I asked if there was something that she wanted to talk about or if there was something on her mind. She remarked that nothing was bothering her and that she was ready for the meeting. I left it at that and went back to focusing on my breakfast.

A few moments later she broke the silence and commented that she had spent most of the previous night surfing news channels. She said that she had never seen so many channels of news running continuously 24 hours a day. I asked her what channels she was watching. After I heard her responses, I said something along the lines of, "Oh, those are not news channels, those are channels representing opinions or providing infotainment."

She looked perplexed and asked what I meant. I went on to say that those channels are not news. They do not report on the developments of the day in an objective manner. The editors and owners of those channels select and present stories that are aligned with their views to make the story more interesting to their audience in order to increase viewership, and ultimately, increase advertising revenue. She seemed taken aback. She asked why they called themselves news channels. I said that I had no answer for that question, but that I knew that they were not reporting the news.

Upon reflection after the conversation, I realized that I intuitively knew that broadcast and cable media companies had changed, but I had not internalized how much they had moved away from presenting objective news and reporting and toward influencing and shaping opinions with a focus on revenue generation. Since 2008 this trend has intensified and increased in its move away from reporting the news objectively.

Media companies and organizations are not the only entities that have moved away from their duty to serve the public good in an open and transparent manner. In the past 50 years, the US government has not been as honest and forthcoming as they have needed to be, and US schools are influenced by local and national organizations that want to further their perspectives, ideas, and agendas by influencing, and in some cases replacing, the entire school curriculum. Organizations write, speak, and espouse different realities based on "alternative facts."

There are not multiple realities based on alternative facts because facts are facts; there cannot be multiples of them. No matter how much people are misled or comforted by a constructed narrative, there is only one objective reality and one true set of facts. Unless a person is insane, deluded, or on psychotropic drugs—then, of course, there are many realities.

This is a sad state of affairs. Organizations, groups, and companies promote their agendas over the good of society.

4.2.2 *Citizenship and our duty to the objective truth*

A good friend of mine, Joe Ray,[2] a Phoenix-based artist and philosopher, has said to me on multiple occasions, "Having voices inside your head is not a problem, until you start listening to them."

It is generally accepted that we should all be positive, proactive citizens working toward the greater good of mankind and our world. We all, as individuals, should be striving each day to make our lives and the lives of all people better.

In ancient Greece, "every citizen was required to participate or suffer punishment. . . . In Athenian democracy, all citizens pulled their weight . . . citizens were free to express their opinions and cast their votes . . . Athenian democracy depended on every citizen fulfilling his role. All citizens were expected to vote, but they were also expected to serve in the government if necessary. In Athens, the people governed, and the majority ruled. All citizens had equal rights and powers."[3]

---

[2] "Joe Ray: In his own words," *Phoenix Art Museum*, Sept. 29, 2020, https://phxart.org/blog/joe-ray/.

[3] "Ancient Greece: 5b. Democracy is Born," *Ancient Civilizations*, cited Dec. 30, 2021, https://www.ushistory.org/civ/5b.asp.

The definitions of citizenship in ancient Greece, revolutionary era America, and numerous other periods of history are admittedly problematic in that they limited citizenship by race, gender, and economic status. But even those definitions required democracy's participants to be inherently interested in the greater good.

In reality, that requirement is too much for many people. They are tired from work, from their responsibilities to their spouse and children, from their financial responsibilities, from their desire to match their life to the fabulous lives of people that they see on social media, and more. But those of us who want to push through the weariness are driving toward and building a better future for ourselves, our children, and even the people who cannot be bothered. We do not need everyone to be part of this movement—small, motivated minorities can make this happen. And when we succeed, all humanity will benefit.

The next section will look at the current state of trust in society today. Trust is one of the fundamental behavioral elements needed to understand the path to engaging with and managing our data in a positive and proactive manner.

4.3   *Trust in government*

When I was an adolescent, it seemed the majority of people trusted our system of government or democracy—the US government, the media, our schools, and most of the institutions that make up American society—to do what was in the best interest of us as individuals, of the country, and of the world. This was one aspect of what was referred to as *American exceptionalism.*[4]

"The erosion of public trust in government began in the 1960s. The share [of the US population] saying they could trust the federal government to do the right thing nearly always or most of the time reached an all-time high of 77% in 1964. Within a decade—a period that included the Vietnam War, civil unrest, and the Watergate scandal—trust had fallen by more than half, to 36%. By the end of the 1970s, only about a quarter of Americans felt that they could trust the government at least most of the time" (figure 4.1).[5] As trust in government has eroded, partisanship and division in the US government and national governments around the world has steadily increased and has been in ascendancy over the past few decades.

In 2017 the Pew Research Center asked people about their satisfaction with the functioning of their governments. When the responses and data were analyzed, the results illustrated that "Publics around the globe are generally unhappy with the functioning of their nations' political systems. Across the 36 countries asked the question, a global median of 46% say they are very or somewhat satisfied with the way their democracy is working, compared with 52% who are not too or not at all satisfied."[6]

[4] Stephen M. Walt, "The Myth of American Exceptionalism," *Foreign Policy*, Oct. 11, 2011, https://foreignpolicy.com/2011/10/11/the-myth-of-american-exceptionalism/.

[5] "Beyond distrust: How Americans view their government," *Pew Research Center*, Nov. 23, 2015, https://www.pewresearch.org/politics/2015/11/23/1-trust-in-government-1958-2015/.

[6] "Globally, broad support for representative and direct democracy," *Pew Research Center*, Oct. 16, 2017, https://www.pewresearch.org/global/2017/10/16/many-unhappy-with-current-political-system/.

Public trust in the federal government has been low for more than a decade

% who say they trust the federal government to do what is right just about always/most of the time

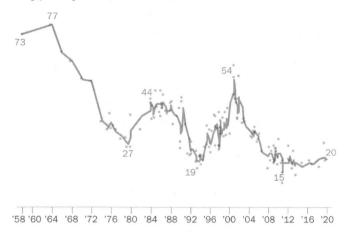

Note: From 1976-2020 the trend line represents a three-survey moving average.
Source: Survey of U.S. adults conducted July 27-Aug. 2, 2020.
Trend sources: Pew Research Center's American Trends Panel (2020), Pew Research Center phone surveys (2019 and earlier), National Election Studies, Gallup, ABC/Washington Post, CBS/New York Times, and CNN polls. See appendix for details.

PEW RESEARCH CENTER

Figure 4.1 Public trust in the US government, 1958–2020[7]

In recent years, trust in government has been highly correlated to personal and ideological alignment with the current governing party and the economic health of the country and a person's household. "The status of the economy is strongly related to people's trust in their government. Publics that have experienced a higher level of economic growth over the past five years tend to have more confidence in their national government to do the right thing for their country. For example, in India, where the economy has grown on average by 6.9% since 2012, 85% trust their national government. Meanwhile, just 26% of Italians have confidence in their government; their economy has contracted over the past five years (–0.5% average GDP growth)."[8]

Partisanship in recent years has led to the election of a number of autocratic-leaning leaders, including in the United States. Autocratic leaders tend to be interested in shielding the public from data, making government operations more opaque and generally trend toward secrecy rather than openness. All characteristics that are anathema to what we are seeking: more open access, deeper understanding, transparency, and an ability to freely engage with all sorts and sources of data.

While this trend toward autocratic governance is concerning, it appears that the majority of people remain resolute in the belief that a representative democracy is the

[7] Ibid.
[8] Ibid.

best form of government. "A global median of 78% back government by elected representatives. But the intensity of this support varies significantly between nations. Roughly six-in-ten Ghanaians (62%), 54% of Swedes and 53% of Senegalese and Tanzanians hold the view that representative democracy is very good. Just 8% of Brazilians and 9% of Mexicans agree. The only countries where there is significantly strong opposition to representative democracy are Colombia (24% say it is very bad) and Tunisia (23% very bad)."[9]

Representative democracy is the best form of government for ensuring we have the freedom to have a voice in how we and others manage our data. Democracy looks to be the preferred form of government in the future, but we must be diligent and ensure that our governments serve and protect our interests and rights. This extends to all aspects of our data.

While many Americans have historically espoused an approach to data management that leans more toward the free market or laissez-faire orientation than toward government regulation, it appears that the longer-term trend is moving against this general view.

A recent survey conducted by the Schar School at George Mason University for the *Washington Post* found that in the past nine years, public sentiment has not only flipped, but increasingly agrees with the need for government to intervene in data and privacy related matters regarding how companies collect, store, manage, and use our data (see figure 4.2).[10]

```
10. Do you think the government should do more to regulate how Internet companies
handle privacy issues, or should the government NOT get more involved in this?

            Should       Should NOT get      No
            do more      more involved     opinion
11/22/21      64             35               1

Compare to:

            Should       Should NOT get      No
            do more      more involved     opinion
2/12/12*      38             56               7
*Pew Research Center
```

Figure 4.2   Public sentiment regarding government involvement in data regulation[11]

In the next section we will examine the current state of trust in relation to commercial companies.

---

[9] Ibid.

[10] "Washington Post-Schar School tech poll, Nov. 4–22, 2021," updated on Dec. 22, 2021, cited on Dec. 31, 2021, http://mng.bz/X5zG.

[11] Ibid.

4.4   Trust in business and business leaders

While the institutions of business are the most trusted in our society today, that is like saying that they are the least bad of the bunch. It is not a position of distinction. Business leaders or CEOs are currently not held in high regard but *are expected* to act in ways that are in the best interests of people and society.

According to the 2021 Edelman Trust Barometer survey, global leadership at many levels is viewed as less trustworthy than in previous years. "With a growing Trust gap and trust declines worldwide, people are looking for leadership and solutions as they reject talking heads who they deem not credible. . . . In particular, CEO's credibility is at all-time lows in several countries, including Japan (18 percent) and France (22 percent), making the challenge for CEO leaders even more acute as they try to address today's problems."[12]

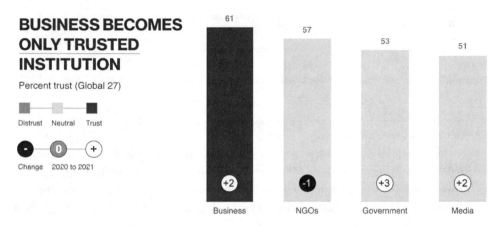

Figure 4.3   Trust in institutions fell in 2021.[13]

Contrary to how we treat, talk about, and perceive CEOs, they are simply people who find themselves in positions of influence and power, often more based on opportunity than ability. Many CEOs will not rise to meet the occasion, and we should not be surprised at their lack of charity, clarity, honesty, intellect, interest, empathy, or their ability to master the skills needed to lead during these tumultuous times. With that said, CEOs are in positions of responsibility and accountability that they freely, and in many cases eagerly, signed up for, and we, both as individuals and collectively, should hold them to their end of the deal.

CEOs are well paid, sometimes exalted, lavishly praised, and generally provided with and treated to a *very* comfortable lifestyle. We should expect them to deliver on all elements of corporate performance, including being ethical, honest, and *competent*

---

[12]"2021 Edelman Trust Barometer," *Edelman*, cited Dec. 28, 2021, https://www.edelman.com/trust/ 2021-trust-barometer.

[13]Ibid. The Trust Index is the average percent trust in NGOs, business, government, and media.

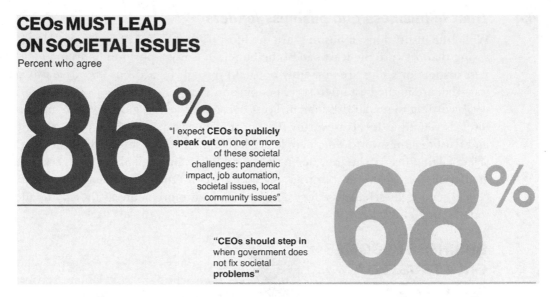

Figure 4.4   CEOs and companies are expected to lead, especially when government does not.[14]

when it comes to the handling of our data. This is not too much to ask. Let's raise our expectations of this group.

CEOs lead companies, and trust in companies, governments, media, and all tracked organizations have hit an all-time low in the 21 years that the Edelman Trust Index has been calculated. CEOs like to represent that the responsibility lies with them. As Harry S. Truman said, "The buck stops here."[15] Great, let's press them on this position as it relates to our data.

In general, we should be aware of and interested in what companies are doing with and to our data, but we specifically need to be more interested in and concerned with technology companies and what they are doing with our data. In the next section we'll look more closely at technology firms.

4.4.1   *Trust in technology companies*

Most people interface with technologies from a handful of companies that collect and generate data about us, our children, our family members, our friends, and our interconnected activities as we go about our daily lives. Currently, the level of trust in these companies is very low to non-existent, but people continue to buy, subscribe to, and use these products and online services.

A story in the *Washington Post* outlines the array of technology products found in a typical American household: "You'll find all the usual technology suspects inside Mary

---

[14]Ibid.

[15]Harry S. Truman Library and Museum, cited Dec. 29, 2021, https://www.trumanlibrary.gov/education/trivia/buck-stops-here-sign.

Veselka's Pearland, Tex., home. There's her iPhone, a school-issued iPad for her young daughter and the latest boxes delivered from Amazon. The full-time mother has an active Facebook account and a TikTok account and sitting in her living room is an Echo speaker, its Alexa voice assistant always ready to add items to her shopping list or turn off the lights."[16]

Veselka explains in the interview that she has a low level of trust in technology companies but feels as if she needs to be connected via the online services and products dotted around her house. "Like many Americans, Veselka's daily life is saturated with the products and services pushed by big technology companies, paid and free. And like many Americans, she simultaneously does not trust the businesses or the people running them when it comes to privacy issues, but can't simply shake them off, either. She doesn't like the way Facebook collects her personal data to target ads, or the kinds of videos YouTube offers to her child, and she suspects that her devices are always listening."[17]

As described in the preceding excerpt, a significant portion of the population feels that they have little to no choice but to use the technology and online services on offer today. Technology companies have not done a good job of developing responsible data management processes, systems, and environments that enable end users to access, modify, delete, and proactively manage their data on the platforms. The feelings of having no real options and the fact that companies are perceived to be using and abusing data on a widespread basis has led to a widespread feeling of distrust of technology companies.

When you look at the data in figure 4.5, it is obvious that overall trust in technology companies is quite low. Only one company has a majority of people who trust it to handle their personal data, Amazon at 53%. Facebook stands out with a substantial portion of the population having a low level of trust. Look closely at the distrust scores for Meta's properties (Facebook, WhatsApp, and Instagram)—they are significantly higher than those of other large, well-known technology companies. None of the Meta platforms even reach a 5% score under the category "Trust a great deal." It is noteworthy that Meta's competitors TikTok and YouTube are even more distrusted. We need to reexamine our relationships with technology companies, our data, and how we access and manage our data.

---

[16]Heather Kelly and Emily Guskin, "Americans widely distrust Facebook, TikTok and Instagram with their data, poll finds," *Washington Post*, Dec. 22, 2021, https://www.washingtonpost.com/technology/2021/12/22/tech-trust-survey/.

[17]Ibid.

```
9. (AMONG INTERNET USERS) How much do you trust each of the following companies or
services to responsibly handle your personal information and data on your Internet
activity?

Summary table - 11/22/21
```

| | | ------- Trust -------- | | --- Trust less ---- | | | |
	NET	A great deal	A good amount	NET	Not much	Not at all	No opinion
a. Amazon	53	14	39	40	25	15	7
b. Apple	44	18	26	40	21	18	16
c. Google	48	14	34	47	28	19	4
d. Microsoft	43	10	33	42	26	16	15
e. Facebook	20	4	16	72	32	40	8
f. Instagram	19	3	16	60	30	31	20
g. TikTok	12	2	10	63	23	39	25
h. WhatsApp	15	3	12	53	19	34	32
i. YouTube	35	7	28	53	31	22	12

Figure 4.5   Trust in technology companies' management of personal data[18]

4.4.2   Why do people feel they need to be connected to technology?

Most people believe that technology is ubiquitous by nature. That is not a necessary state of being, but it is an accepted fact by a wide range of people. We have had Google since 1998 and Facebook since 2004. A generation has grown up knowing only a world where these platforms are part of daily life. This generation and the one following them see these products and services as part of the ecosystem of life.

Being connected is a human need. We are social animals. Mobile devices and online social media platforms exploit this need and weaponize it against the majority of the population, partially by using our own data against us. The majority of the population uses what is offered and marketed to them, and if it is "free," people are more drawn to it than options where they must pay.

---

[18]"Washington Post-Schar School tech poll, Nov. 4–22, 2021," updated on Dec. 22, 2021, cited on Dec. 31, 2021, http://mng.bz/X5zG.

This brings us to a salient question. What combination of government, business, and philanthropic organizations will drive positive change, creative and responsible innovation, leadership, and governance? The public is "open to new alternatives if they're presented. That sounds like a golden opportunity for a round of entrepreneurs to come up with new ways of interaction that don't rely on sucking up more and more data in exchange for free access to digital services. In [the near future], we'll see new forms of social interaction being built on the blockchain, as well as formidable new search [options] and e-commerce alternatives, that will slowly leech at the foundations of the larger operations."[19]

One of the major problems in the technology market is that there are not enough compelling options for the population to choose from. We need a wave of innovation to help change this. We need entrepreneurs, innovators, sources of risk capital, and government initiatives to spur innovation that will provide new options for people to engage with. New companies that manage data in new and novel ways. Ways that enable individuals and companies to benefit from using data.

As we move down the ladder of trust, we finally arrive at the companies that are least trusted today: media companies.

4.4.3 Trust in media companies

Many media companies have turned away from the news business and converted their previous news operations into infotainment offerings or mouthpieces for corporate or special interests. At the same time, social media and search engine companies have been allowed to move into media operations with none of the traditional governance and oversight functions applied to their operations. Facebook is clearly the most high-profile company that has used data extensively, applying artificial intelligence in numerous ways.

David Kirkpatrick, a long-time Facebook observer, writes,

The enormous set of unseemly revelations known as the Facebook Papers show, among other things, that Facebook is a global media company that does not bear its associated responsibilities. . . .

Traditional media companies, unlike Facebook, are required by law and tradition to bear responsibility for the content they present to viewers. Internet companies, by contrast, got an exemption in the now-notorious Section 230 of the Communications Decency Act of 1996, which says content created by users is not the responsibility of web platforms. Facebook has applied that logic of non-responsibility to speech and content distributed all over the world.

But Facebook doesn't just provide a neutral window for content created by friends and organizations you follow. It curates that content and shows it to you selectively, in the order it chooses—in a way that maximizes revenue. What it shows you is its willful decision.[20]

---

[19]Kara Swisher, "Trump's Social Media Return—and What Else to Expect in 2022," *New York Times*, Dec. 30, 2021, https://www.nytimes.com/2021/12/30/opinion/trump-facebook-matrix.html.

[20]David Kirkpatrick, "Facebook, the Imperialist Media Company," *Technonomy*, Oct. 29, 2021, https://techonomy.com/2021/10/facebook-imperialist-media-company/.

The public, pundits, and a few government officials have called for a move to insert human editors into the process of posting content on social media platforms. This is a call that is too little, too late. Social media platforms do not work the way that newspapers and television stations did in the past.

The long-term problem in having no guiding principle other than maximizing making money in the news/media business is that objective reporting turns into opinion, facts become meaningless, our data is used to manipulate messaging and targeting, and trust is lost. This is the end result no matter who is making the editorial choices about what stories, messages, or posts to display and in what order. This is the outcome when human editors are put in this position, and it happens even more quickly and stridently when the job is left to algorithms.

CEOs and company leadership are responsible for the falling trust levels relating to the media industry and across all media types. All of the media types listed in figure 4.6 are the products of companies. Media does not exist in a vacuum. Media is a product just as financial services and automobiles are products.

TRUST IN ALL INFORMATION SOURCES AT RECORD LOWS

Percent trust in each source for general news and information

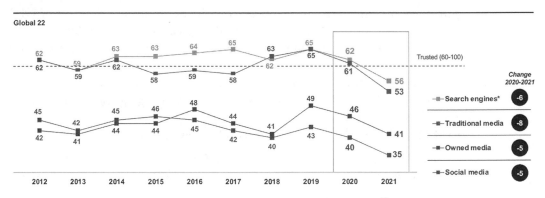

Figure 4.6   Trend of individual trust levels in all tracked information sources[21]

We as a society, and our respective governments and their agencies and ministries, have failed in how we view, manage, and regulate media. Governments have been hornswoggled by online media and commerce companies. These companies have sold governments on the concept that online media and online transactions are fundamentally different than those same operations in the physical world; that assertion has proven to be untrue.

Of course, we as a society and a global community have benefited from the establishment and ubiquity of the internet and the near friction-free environments that

[21]"2021 Edelman Trust Barometer," *Edelman,* cited Dec. 28, 2021, https://www.edelman.com/trust/2021-trust-barometer.

have been created on top of the internet, and now that process is complete. Governments need to step in and regulate the operation and offerings from online media companies in the same way that they do with media companies in the physical world.

NEWS ORGANIZATIONS SEEN AS BIASED

Percent who agree

Journalists and reporters are purposely trying to mislead people by saying things they know are false or gross exaggerations	Most news organizations are more concerned with supporting an ideology or political position than with informing the public	The media is not doing well at being objective and non-partisan

			Strongest agreement that media is not doing well in:	
		⊥	Japan	80
			S. Korea	77
			Colombia	76
Global 27	Global 27	Global 24	Argentina	75
			Italy	75
59%	**59%**	**61%**	Spain	73
			Brazil	72
			UK	69
			*Nigeria	67
			Mexico	66

Figure 4.7   The majority of people do not believe the media is an honest or objective broker of information.[22]

> *Americans largely think tech giants are too big and should be regulated, and mostly don't believe the news media is good for U.S. society, according to a poll from YouGov and the Center for Growth and Opportunity . . . :*
>
> - *63% of baby boomers polled said the government should regulate social media, while 40% of Generation Z agreed.*
> - *66% of those polled say big tech companies are too big, although less than half said they think the government should break them up.*
> - *There's a range of opinions on which tech companies are most trustworthy: 40% of 996 people polled said they "completely distrust" Facebook on handling personal data. For Google, that number was 22%; for Amazon, it was 14%; for Microsoft, it was 15%.*
> - *69% of those polled say news companies and media outlets should be fined for reporting biased or inaccurate information.[23]*

What is clear is that business leaders, media companies, tech companies, and especially social media companies are not trusted by their users in the US and on a global basis. What is less clear is what to do about the current situation.

---

[22]"2021 Edelman Trust Barometer," *Edelman*, cited Dec. 28, 2021, https://www.edelman.com/trust/2021-trust-barometer.

[23]Ashley Gold, "Exclusive: Poll shows wide distrust of tech, media," *Axios*, Feb. 4, 2021, http://mng.bz/yd5G.

4.5   *Trust is lost; time for a change*

The good news in all of this is that people are getting fed up and motivated enough to demand change. The current environment we find ourselves in is a product of change, societal evolution, growth, innovation, and more. Let's drive change in a direction that benefits us as individuals and humankind as a whole. Going backward or returning to some poorly recalled past is not an option.

Heather Cox Richardson, an American historian and professor of history at Boston College, said, "One of the curses of history is that we cannot go back and change the course leading to disasters, no matter how much we might wish to. The past has its own terrible inevitability. But it is never too late to change the future."[24] Describing our current state of affairs, relating to how our data is used, as a disaster is not over-stating the situation. When companies aggressively and intentionally take something that is yours and co-opt it to make a substantial amount of money for a small number of people, that is a significant problem. We may disagree on the severity and urgency of the problem, and we may disagree on the solutions to the problem, but most people do agree that, fundamentally, this is a problem. It will only get worse if we do not act and if we do not engage our governments, the financial system, and our agents of change in our global societies. Just as the deteriorating global climate needs urgent action, so does our data environment.

A growing percentage of the general population expect to be part of the changes that we want and need (see figure 4.8). People no longer agree that free email and free search are enough compensation for their data and insights into their every move

CONSUMERS AND EMPLOYEES
EXPECTED TO HAVE A SEAT AT THE TABLE
Percent who agree

68% **62**% **50**% of those who are employed

Consumers …   Employees …

**have the power to force
corporations to change**

I am more likely now than a year ago to voice my objections to management or **engage in workplace protest**

Figure 4.8   **The majority of people expect to have a say in what and how we change.**[25]

---

[24]Heather Cox Richardson, "December 28, 2021," *Letters from an American*, https://heathercoxrichardson .substack.com/p/december-28-2021.

[25]"2021 Edelman Trust Barometer," *Edelman*, cited Dec. 28, 2021, https://www.edelman.com/trust/ 2021-trust-barometer.

and purchase, every turn they make in their car, every drop of cold medicine they take, and every call they make to check in on their family members. The percentage of people in the general population who expect change is rising and exceeds the majority in well-defined and known communities and groups. As noted previously, we do not need an absolute majority—we do not need every person on the planet to agree that change is needed—we just need a motivated and vocal minority to increase the momentum of this movement and change. We need to put pressure on the system where it will do the most good.

People have started to take individual action; figure 4.9 indicates that a significant number of people are taking the actions they can on their own to limit the data that online companies can collect about them. But we have to be realistic. These changes are limited to what can be modified on the user's local computer. Chapter 1 discussed how our data traverses a public or private wireless network, our local internet service provider, the computing infrastructure of the internet, the systems involved in online commerce, media, and other companies, and the mobile devices of the users that the data is being sent to and shared with. All of these waypoints are still locations where our data potentially resides on a transitory, semi-permanent, or virtually permanent basis and where it can be accessed and used freely by other individuals with benign or malignant intent, companies, governments, and more.

```
12. (AMONG INTERNET USERS) Have you, personally, done any of the following to limit
the information websites, search engines or apps gather about you?

Summary table - 11/22/21

                                    Yes
a. Changed your browser settings     39
b. Deleted your web history          56
c. Changed the privacy settings
   of websites, such as not
   allowing tracking                 57
d. Altered the privacy settings
   on your phone or apps             50
e. Used a private browsing
   setting such as "incognito
   mode"                             37
f. Used a virtual private
   network (VPN) to protect
   your privacy                      26
NET any:                             78
```

Figure 4.9   Individual actions related to limiting online information collection[26]

While it is a positive sign that individuals are not alone in these views and feelings, the actions of individuals are not enough. We can, and do, have a consensus that our data

---

[26]"Washington Post-Schar School tech poll, Nov. 4–22, 2021," updated on Dec. 22, 2021, cited on Dec. 31, 2021, http://mng.bz/X5zG.

is being exploited, and we are being manipulated in ways that we do not agree with, and we are frustrated by this situation, but that does not mean that we have a consensus about what needs to be done.

4.6   *Technology and media companies are making bank from your data*

There are portions of the population that feel government regulation is not needed and that the companies themselves can regulate their activities related to data collection and subsequent use, but the 2020 revenue numbers reported by Google and Facebook tell a different story: "The biggest goal of collecting data is to serve up narrowly targeted ads. Two companies dominate. Google earned $147 billion in revenue from advertising in 2020, or 80 percent of its total, while Facebook earned $84 billion in revenue from advertising, or 98 percent of its total."[27]

Any company that is earning the vast majority of its revenue from a specific activity, advertising in this case, will not voluntarily and proactively change its operations to affect those revenue streams. It is rare that it has ever happened, and it will not happen in this case. I can state with complete certainty that voluntary change is not forthcoming from any of these companies. The only way forward from where we are today is a combination of individual actions, which are taking place already. We also need national, state, and local governments to act. We need watchdog groups and think tanks to examine the current business models and data ecosystems and make suggestions and proposals for innovation and new business models. We need investment firms to make bets on, and invest in, new companies that will disrupt the status quo of today.

4.6.1   *What is the value of data, and how much can it mean to each individual?*

Let's take a moment to compare the value of the various sources of data that we create (see chapter 3 for the full list of data that we create) to the well-established business model that few understand. Think about your favorite music artist. It could be a band, a songwriter, a music publisher, or anyone in the creation and production of music. Do you believe that they deserve the royalties that they are paid each and every time one of their compositions is played? Most people do believe that those artists deserve to be paid for their contributions and creations.

For the sake of our discussion, let's say that an artist is paid a tenth of a penny each time a song is played. That is not much money, but very popular artists receive millions of dollars for their efforts.[28] I believe that our data has the same type of intrinsic value and that we should be paid each and every time a data element that we have created is used. Perhaps we are paid a millionth of a penny, or perhaps we set the rate we are paid according to the type of organization that wants to use our data. We will delve into this topic more deeply later in the book, but for now I just want to make the comparison to

---

[27]"Washington Post-Schar School tech poll, Nov. 4–22, 2021," updated on Dec. 22, 2021, cited on Dec. 31, 2021, http://mng.bz/X5zG.

[28]Lee Ann Obringer, "How Music Royalties Work," *How Stuff Works*, https://entertainment.howstuffworks.com/music-royalties.htm.

music royalties. In practical terms, our data has value. We should be paid when our data is used in a manner that delivers revenue to any commercial organization. I believe fervently that this idea, once it takes hold, will resonate widely with the general public.

The concept is being discussed today, and one name that is used to refer to the idea in practice is a *data dividend.* How would you like to get a check each month or every year for the use of your data? I would. Each time a royalty check arrives in my bank account for the sales of my books, I smile.

Now, let's take this a step further. I believe individuals should be empowered to, and should be able to, easily set the price of our data for each industry, company, and application. That is an idea that is worth developing, don't you think? Again, I will outline and describe this complete idea and system later in the book.

For now, let's turn our attention to governmental efforts to change how our data is collected, managed, and leveraged.

4.7   Governmental regulations

The changes required to govern and manage our data cannot and will not come from companies, large or small. Change can be discussed by academics, not-for-profit organizations, and individuals, but change cannot begin with them. Change of the required scale can only begin with international and national governments. Let's examine the changes that are underway at the international and national levels.

4.7.1   The European Union

We introduced the topic of the European Union's General Data Protection Regulation (GDPR) and their nascent Data Governance Act and Data Act legislation in chapter 2.

I vividly recall the reaction in the United States when the European Union (EU) announced in 2016 that they would take up the issue of data protection and begin the process of defining rules, regulations, and laws related to the collection, creation, and use of the personal data of EU citizens. The articles written and published about the proposed GDPR legislation were scathing and used a wide range of tactics ranging from merely listing the required changes in business processes and practices to scaremongering and fantastic pronouncements about American rights being usurped and the sovereignty of the US government being diminished.

The Federalist Society, a conservative US institute, offered this assessment as a call to bring Americans out against the GDPR: "If the GDPR were adopted in the U.S., it would likely violate the First Amendment, as the requirements for data processing are so onerous that they would be found to limit expression."[29] If anything will stir American emotions, especially in the conservative portion of the US population, it is the hint that any proposed idea or legislation, especially if suggested by a foreign body or

---

[29]Roslyn Layton and Julian McLendon, "The GDPR: What It Really Does and How the U.S. Can Chart a Better Course," *The Federalist Society Review,* vol. 19, Oct 29, 2018, https://fedsoc.org/commentary/publications/the-gdpr-what-it-really-does-and-how-the-u-s-can-chart-a-better-course.

government, will infringe on the rights of American citizens established and detailed in the US Constitution.

The following example is more factual and simply calls out a change that is required by all US companies that will be interacting with EU citizens: "For example, say a Chicago-based software company is looking to run a campaign in France and has set up a webpage to collect email addresses for a white paper. At the very least, the company will need a checkbox—without a default 'x' in it—accompanied by clear language about what it will be doing with these email addresses. And it's not allowable to ask the user to click on a link to a long 'terms and conditions' document filled with legalese."[30]

THE GDPR AND ITS FOUNDATIONAL PRINCIPLES

Six years later, the GDPR is not the nightmare that it was portrayed to be in the US media and by companies that still do not want these types of changes to proliferate around the world. The GDPR is a well-constructed, easy to read law that

> . . . *codifies standards for data processing and collection, creating sweeping rules governing the use of EU data even outside the borders of the EU. . . . every company must start with the following considerations when working toward GDPR compliance:*
>
> - *Expanded disclosure—Companies must offer a good description of what data they collect, for what purpose, and how it is stored and processed. This includes who else the data is shared with, how long the data is stored and how the data is protected.*
> - *User control—Companies must grant users more control over what happens to their data. Users are entitled to a copy of their data, if requested. They can also request their data be deleted, or that amendments be made to incorrect data. Users also have the right to consent as to whether their data is shared with a third-party company for any purposes other than outsourcing processing.*
> - *Downstream compliance—Any third-party companies and service providers must be compliant with GDPR as well; otherwise, the company collecting the data can be held liable. In other words, if you collect user data by the rules of GDPR but outsource processing to a noncompliant company, you could remain on the hook for violations. This includes consideration of third-party cookies and how they might collect and track general data.*[31]

While most companies do not relish the idea of considering new laws and making operational, procedural, and programming and program changes in their systems, it is not onerous or problematic for them to do so. They do it consistently and with regularity. They have to; it is the law, and laws change all the time.

BENEFITS OF THE GDPR

The GDPR has brought a number of changes that have benefited citizens around the world. Few companies have been disadvantaged, few to no firms have gone out of

---

[30] Yaki Faitelson, "Yes, The GDPR Will Affect Your U.S.-Based Business," *Forbes*, Dec. 4, 2017, https://www.forbes.com/sites/forbestechcouncil/2017/12/04/yes-the-gdpr-will-affect-your-u-s-based-business/.

[31] Adam Uzialko, "How GDPR Is Impacting Business and What to Expect in 2020," *Business News Daily*, Feb. 4, 2020, https://www.businessnewsdaily.com/15510-gdpr-in-review-data-privacy.html.

business, and there have been no dire consequences from providing a modicum of access, control, and management to an individual's data by that individual.

The GDPR has proven to be a significant and widespread success. The national governments that comprise the EU—Austria, Belgium, Bulgaria, Croatia, Republic of Cyprus, Czech Republic, Denmark, Estonia, Finland, France, Germany, Greece, Hungary, Ireland, Italy, Latvia, Lithuania, Luxembourg, Malta, Netherlands, Poland, Portugal, Romania, Slovakia, Slovenia, Spain, and Sweden—have proven that the governmental oversight and legislative process works well in considering the rights, implications, laws, and potential positive changes that can be developed and implemented relating to the enhanced and improved stewardship of our personal data.

The "GDPR is just the 'catalyst' that kicked off a tidal wave of global data protection laws. Companies should monitor similar developments around the world. This isn't isolated to EU citizens and California. It's a trend that's going to sweep the world."[32]

BEYOND THE GDPR: THE DATA ACT, THE DATA GOVERNANCE ACT, AND MORE

Currently the EU is working on new legislation based in part on the following precept: "The public sphere needs an 'ecosystem of trust' which could set out objectives of re-usage of data for the common good while protecting individual rights . . . related to data, asserting that the systemic level of data assemblage must be re-conceptualized to reject the data-as-a-commodity view and take public interest into consideration. For data stewardship to achieve its goals, it is necessary to consider the inherent properties of data as commons. . . . [A] public data commons [is] the model that is best suited to secure European rights and values while increasing data sharing at the same time."[33]

The EU has proposed the Data Governance Act including changes in the following areas of how data is collected, protected, stored, managed, and leveraged:

- *Good data management and data sharing will enable industries to develop innovative products and services and will make many sectors of the economy more efficient and sustainable. It is also essential for training AI systems.*
- *With more data available, the public sector can develop better policies, leading to more transparent governance and more efficient public services.*
- *Data-driven innovation will bring benefits for companies and individuals by making our lives and work more efficient through:*
  - *health data: improving personalized treatments, providing better healthcare, and helping cure rare or chronic diseases, saving approximately €120 billion a year in the EU health sector and providing a more effective and quicker response to the global COVID-19 health crisis;*
  - *mobility data: saving more than 27 million hours of public transport users' time and up to €20 billion a year in labor costs of car drivers thanks to real-time navigation;*

---

[32]Ibid.

[33]Jan J. Zygmuntowski, Laura Zoboli, and Paul F. Nemitz "Embedding European values in data governance: a case for public data commons," *Internet Policy Review*, Sept. 30, 2020, https://policyreview.info/articles/analysis/embedding-european-values-data-governance-case-public-data-commons.

> – *environmental data: combatting climate change, reducing CO_2 emissions and fighting emergencies, such as floods and wildfires;*
> – *agricultural data: developing precision farming, new products in the agri-food sector and new services in general in rural areas;*
> – *public administration data: delivering better and more reliable official statistics, and contributing to evidence-based decisions.*[34]

The Data Governance Act is a single step toward creating a data commons that will collect data with the express purpose of using that data for the public good and the good of everyone involved, and not in just some conceptual manner but in a tangible monetary manner for each EU citizen.

On Dec. 6, 2021, the EU announced, "that action at EU or national level is needed on business-to-government data sharing for the public interest, especially for emergencies and crisis management, prevention and resilience. . . . The Data Act will be a major new initiative to ensure fairness by providing better control for data sharing to citizens and businesses. [Through the Data] Act, users will have more control over the data they generate via their smart objects and EU businesses more possibilities to compete and innovate and easily transfer data between service providers. The Data Act will aim at clarifying for EU consumers and businesses who can use and access what data for which purposes. It follows up on and complements the Data Governance Act, which aims to increase trust and facilitate data sharing across the EU."[35]

The Data Act focuses on sharing data between businesses and governments. This is another positive step down the path of creating legal frameworks, operational procedures, methodologies, and best practices toward widespread governance, data sharing, and data use, first between companies and governments and then moving on to data sharing between individuals and companies, individuals and governments, and between individuals.

One portion of the Data Governance Act that is noteworthy are the clauses that outline the creation of Data Intermediaries, also known as data cooperatives or data unions.[36] These are the institutions, organizations, and frameworks that will enable citizens, EU citizens in the beginning, to take control of their data to move, aggregate, share, and monetize the data as they wish.

IMPLICATIONS OF, AND CHANGES DRIVEN BY, EU DATA LEGISLATION

I fully expect that these governance frameworks will be extended to automated systems and artificial intelligence systems as well. These proposed laws and legal frameworks will have a significant effect on the agreements that we as users must sign today to gain access to products and services. These agreements, as currently written for the majority of

[34]"European data governance act," cited Dec. 27, 2021, https://digital-strategy.ec.europa.eu/en/policies/data-governance-act.

[35]"Data Act: Businesses and citizens in favor of a fair data economy," European Commission press release, Dec. 6, 2021, https://digital-strategy.ec.europa.eu/en/news/data-act-businesses-and-citizens-favour-fair-data-economy.

[36]Shiv Malik, "The End of Data Monopolies," *Medium*, Jan. 20, 2022, https://medium.com/pool-data/the-end-of-data-monopolies-b24186ec866c.

companies and applications, illuminate the disadvantageous position companies want us to remain in regarding our data.

Tesla comes to mind. If you buy a Tesla, you are buying a car, but you are also buying a data-generation engine. All that data is shared with Tesla, and you have little to no ability to access, change, or delete that data. You want to buy and drive the Tesla, I get that, but do you want to share every turn you make with the Tesla team? I don't, unless I am getting paid to share that data. Then I might reconsider sharing a small part of my data.

The Data Governance Act and the Data Act are the first steps toward creating an EU data commons. I have spoken with a number of people who have said that this effort will go nowhere. By coincidence, these are the same experts who said that the GDPR would have little to no effect on data collection and use outside the EU, so we can ignore the opinions of these "experts."

In the US, we have had local-number portability for our mobile phone numbers for years. But the EU is way ahead of the US in enabling their citizens to execute and manage total data portability. "Europeans already have the right to port their data out of any company they choose. Article 20 of GDPR gives everyone a right to data portability. The problem is that this right was drafted for the postal age. Article 6.1 subsections (h) and (i) of the Digital Markets Act contains an updated version of GDPR's article 20. It lets businesses and end users port their data from digital giants (or 'gatekeepers' as they are termed in the legislation), to a third party, in real time via an API. In other words, through a few clicks you'll be able to send your data in a continuous stream to any other company you choose."[37]

These early and continued legislative steps by the EU are the path to the future. "And there will be important legislation to help that soon too—just not in the United States. Instead, it will come from Europe, which is trying to finalize the Digital Markets Act and the Digital Services Act, much as they passed the General Data Protection Regulation nearly six years ago. While imperfect, it did set a tone for regulation that has been used worldwide."[38]

Governing leadership will continue to come from the EU. Watch and learn what the future will be by what the EU discusses, drafts, and passes into law. Much of it will benefit the world.

In the next section, we will review the Australian data regulations and laws being drafted and passed.

---

[37]Ibid.

[38]Kara Swisher, "Trump's Social Media Return—and What Else to Expect in 2022," *New York Times*, Dec. 30, 2021, https://www.nytimes.com/2021/12/30/opinion/trump-facebook-matrix.html.

4.7.2 *Australia*

The Australian antitrust regulatory body Australian Competition and Consumer Commission (ACCC) has been leading the way in analyzing and understanding the role of companies in stifling innovation and competition. "Australia has been punching way above its weight when it comes to tech regulation. Its showdown over news on Alphabet's Google and Meta Platforms' Facebook last year [2021] grabbed the world's attention, forcing the two internet companies to back down from threats and agree to deals with traditional media outlets that are worth hundreds of millions of dollars each year. Rod Sims, Australia's chief antitrust official, was the architect of that precedent-setting faceoff. And the big-tech gadfly has made Australia a model for other countries looking to rein in dominant companies without discouraging innovation."[39]

The focus of the Australian efforts has been to find pro-competition compromises between the large tech firms and local companies. One such compromise has Facebook and Google paying local media companies for the local stories produced by those smaller, focused media operations. When you read about the deals, it sounds like something that the big technology and media should have had to do by existing law, but that is not the case.

"[T]he Australian government create[d] rules that would force the two tech giants to pay publishers for news content. The implementation of the 'News Bargaining Code' led to surreal scenes last year [2021]. Facebook threatened a news blackout for Australian users, while Google threatened to cut off search services. Both eventually backed down and drew up deals with major news publishers. Google and Facebook could pay 'well north' of $200 million each year to Australian media companies, Sims said."[40]

It is interesting to hear how the head of a national regulatory body thinks about data and the combination of various data sources. Sims said the following about Google's acquisition of Fitbit, "Fitbit has enough health information that when you combine [that with] Google's information, they will be in a very strong position in the health market. It also gives them [Google] access to the wearables market, which hitherto they haven't been able to get in. It's a transaction that does entrench their market power."[41]

The actions taken by the ACCC and the Australian laws show the way for global regulation that increases healthy competition, strengthens industries and local companies, and checks the power of the global companies without resorting to breaking companies up. Much of the work of the Australian regulators is based on solid data collection, multi-dimensional market analysis, and competitive fairness. That seems like something that we can support on a global basis.

---

[39]Mark DiStefano, "Don't Break Up Big Tech, Says Antitrust Enforcer Who Fought Facebook," *The Information*, Jan. 7, 2022, https://www.theinformation.com/articles/dont-break-up-big-tech-regulate-it-enforcer-who-sparked-australias-facebook-spat.

[40]Ibid.

[41]Ibid.

In the next section we will take a look at the data regulations and laws being drafted in the US.

4.7.3 *The United States*

The US does not have a single and comprehensive federal-level law governing data collection, use, and privacy. Currently, the US relies on a range of laws that are targeted to specific vertical industries or specific instances of data use or specific data types. "There is no single principal data protection legislation in the United States (U.S.). Rather, a jumble of hundreds of laws enacted on both the federal and state levels serve to protect the personal data of U.S. residents. . . . Although there is no general federal legislation impacting data protection, there are a number of federal data protection laws that are sector-specific or focus on particular types of data."[42]

A representative sample of the federal laws include

- The Driver's Privacy Protection Act of 1994 (DPPA) governs the privacy and disclosure of personal information gathered by state Departments of Motor Vehicles.
- The Children's Online Privacy Protection Act (COPPA) prohibits the collection of any information from a child under the age of 13 online and from digitally connected devices and requires the publication of privacy notices and the collection of verifiable parental consent when information from children is being collected.
- The Video Privacy Protection Act (VPPA) restricts the disclosure of rental or sale records of videos or similar audio-visual materials, including online streaming. Similarly, the Cable Communications Policy Act of 1984 includes provisions dedicated to the protection of subscriber privacy.
- The Gramm Leach Bliley Act (GLBA) governs the protection of personal information in the hands of banks, insurance companies, and other companies in the financial service industry.
- The Fair Credit Reporting Act (FCRA), as amended by the Fair and Accurate Credit Transactions Act (FACTA), restricts the use of information with a bearing on an individual's creditworthiness, credit standing, credit capacity, character, general reputation, personal characteristics, or mode of living to determine eligibility for credit, employment, or insurance.
- The Health Information Portability and Accountability Act (HIPAA) protects information held by a covered entity that concerns health status, provision of healthcare, or payment for healthcare that can be linked to an individual. Its Privacy Rule regulates the collection and disclosure of such information. Its Security Rule imposes requirements for securing this data.

---

[42]F. Paul Pittman and Kyle Levenberg, "US Data Protection Laws and Regulations 2021," *ICLG*, chapter 37, USA, June 7, 2021, https://iclg.com/practice-areas/data-protection-laws-and-regulations/usa.

- The Telephone Consumer Protection Act (TCPA) and associated regulations regulate calls and text messages to mobile phones and regulate calls to residential phones that are made for marketing purposes or using automated dialing systems or pre-recorded messages.
- The Family Educational Rights and Privacy Act (FERPA) provides students with the right to inspect and revise their student records for accuracy, while also prohibiting the disclosure of these records or other personal information on the student without the student's or parent's (in some instances) consent.
- The US Privacy Act of 1974 contains rights and restrictions on data held by US government agencies.

To me, this says that the US has numerous laws targeted at very specific use cases that are all unnecessarily complex and hard to understand, interpret, and enforce. The US is behind the curve in enacting comprehensive, clear, easy to understand laws related to the collection, management, and use of our data. This needs to change.

In the US, the situation is no better at the state level. The laws are easier to understand, given that there are very few states (only six at the time of the writing of this book) that have any laws regarding data collection and use (see figure 4.10). Let's look at the few states that have taken steps toward enacting relevant legislation.

US State Privacy Law Comparison

State	Right to Delete?	Right to Access?	Right to Correct?	Private Right of Private Action?	Broad Definition of PII?	Businesses covered	Status
California	Yes	Yes	No	$750/consumer (breaches)	Yes (Probabilistic)	Revenues over $25 million	In effect : 1/1/2020
New York	Yes	Yes	Yes	$750/consumer	Yes	All	Pending
Maryland	Yes	Yes	No	No. (Only through AG.)	Yes (Probabilistic)	Over $25 million	Pending
Massachusetts	Yes	Yes	No	$750/consumer	Yes (Probabilistic)	Over $10 million	Pending
Hawaii	Yes	Yes	No	No	Yes	All	Pending
North Dakota	No	Yes	No	Limited	No	Over $25 million	Pending

Figure 4.10   US state privacy law comparison[43]

[43]Andy Green, "Complete Guide to Privacy Laws in the US," *Inside Out Security Blog*, updated April 4, 2021, https://www.varonis.com/blog/us-privacy-laws/.

CALIFORNIA

Given the inattention and inertia from the US federal government, it is not surprising that states have acted on their own. California is leading the way in this area and has drafted their own data privacy laws.

"In 2018, the California Consumer Privacy Act (CCPA) was signed into law. Its goal is to extend consumer privacy protections to the Internet. It's not an exaggeration to say the CCPA is the most comprehensive Internet-focused data privacy legislation in the US, and with no equivalent at the federal level."[44]

"Under the CCPA, consumers have a right to access through a data subject access request (DSAR) the categories and specific pieces of personal information held by covered businesses. Businesses can't sell consumers' personal information without providing an online notice ("a clean and conspicuous link") and giving individuals an opportunity to opt-out."[45]

In many ways the CCPA mirrors many of the provisions of the GDPR. The CCPA

- Includes the "right to delete" consumer personal information on request. The CCPA also gives consumers a limited right of action to sue if they're the victim of a data breach.

- Enumerates a very broad definition of personal information: "information that identifies, relates to, describes, is capable of being associated with, or could reasonably be linked, directly or indirectly, with a particular consumer or household." This is a very broad definition of personal data and is similar to the GDPR's definition.

- Contains a long list of identifiers it considers personal information, including biometric, geolocation, email, browsing history, employee data, and more.

- Introduces the concept of "probabilistic identifiers." Attorneys will be debating what this means, but the current consensus is that it is a collection of data elements that provides a greater than 50% chance of positively identifying a unique individual: "[A] Probabilistic Identifier means information that can be used to identify a consumer or device to a degree of certainty more probable than not."[46]

  This portion of the CCPA will need to be further refined and defined. It is too broad and too vague. As an analytics professional, I can use a small number of data elements to define and identify an individual. More work is needed to make this part of the CCPA work in practicality.

Beyond California, several US states are drafting their own regulations to give citizens increased control over their personal data. While most of these state-level proposals use the CCPA as a framework, there are differences. Let's take a quick look at proposals

---

[44]Ibid.

[45]Ibid.

[46]Aloni Cohen, "Rethinking Probabilistic Identifiers for the CCPA," *Aspen Tech Policy Hub*, October 2019, https://www.aspentechpolicyhub.org/wp-content/uploads/2019/10/Po-Op_CCPA_-v4.pdf.

from the five additional US states that have possible new laws actively moving through the legislative process.

MASSACHUSETTS

The proposed Massachusetts law contains a significant amount of common language with the CCPA:

- Consumer access to personal information
- Right to delete
- Explicit notification of privacy rights, and a chance to opt-out of sales of data to third parties
- A broad definition of personal information
- Probabilistic identifiers

There are a few important divergences from the CCPA, which include the right for consumers to sue for any violation of the proposed Massachusetts law. Individuals "need not suffer a loss of money or property as a result of the violation" to bring an action. There is substantial potential exposure of Massachusetts companies to class-action lawsuits: plaintiffs can recover up to $750 per consumer per data breach or incident.

NEW YORK

New York's proposal contains some of the hallmarks of the CCPA. There's a right to delete and request personal information. The definition of personal information— "any information related to an identified or identifiable person"—includes a very extensive list of identifiers: biometric, email addresses, network information, and more.

Unlike California, and similar to Massachusetts, New York's act has a private right of action for any violation of the law. Also, the law applies to all businesses without any revenue threshold, which differs from all other states.

The New York bill, though, only requires businesses to disclose to consumers the broad categories of information shared to third parties. Under some circumstances, consumers would have the right to request copies of specific information shared.

Another key difference in the proposed New York law is that the law imposes the role of data fiduciary, forcing all New York businesses to be legally responsible for the consumer data they hold. The New York act takes a very expansive view: "exercise the duty of care, loyalty and confidentiality expected of a fiduciary with respect to securing the personal data of a consumer against a privacy risk; and shall act in the best interests of the consumer, without regard to the interests of the entity, controller or data broker."

The New York act also gives consumers the ability to correct inaccurate information, making it closer in spirit to the EU's GDPR. None of the other US state laws, including California, go that far. The bottom line is that when the New York law comes into force, an individual owns their data.

HAWAII

Hawaii's law is similar to the CCPA, offering all of the same major rights and protections. However, while CCPA explicitly applies to websites that conduct business in the state of California, Hawaii's bill has no similar clause.

In theory, websites based anywhere in the world could violate Hawaii's law if they don't offer adequate protection as outlined in the bill. However, the bill is likely to be amended in a later draft to focus solely on Hawaiian-based websites.

MARYLAND

Maryland's bill is another with the potential to expand on the scope of the CCPA in some areas. Businesses will have similar obligations to disclose information usage, though to a lesser degree than under the CCPA. And like California and Massachusetts, there's also the use of a "probabilistic identifier" to refer to a certain type of personal information.

Maryland's bill goes beyond the scope of the CCPA when it comes to disclosing third-party involvement. Under the CCPA, companies only have to disclose if consumer information is being sold to a third party, but in accordance with Maryland's bill, companies would have to disclose any information that is passed on to third parties, even if that data is transferred for free. This bill also prohibits websites from knowingly disclosing any personal information collected about children.

NORTH DAKOTA

North Dakota's bill is the most lightweight bill on this list. The only significant clause would completely restrict websites from passing on any information to third parties without the consent of users. There is no right to have information removed or deleted once consent has been granted.

4.8 Effect of data laws around the globe

As you can see, in the six years since the GDPR has been enacted, the EU law has had a significant effect on the world of data and laws regulating how governments and companies can collect, store, manage, share, and use an individual's data. People who continue to say that the GDPR is only a European phenomenon are simply not paying attention.

The GDPR is being used as a blueprint for consumer data protection on a global basis. The six US states that have legislation in process are only the first movers; more states and more national governments will take this up as a priority. I expect that new laws at the state level will accelerate in momentum.

I want to be clear: this chapter, and this book, is not an exhaustive or comprehensive survey of data legislation on the books or in process. There are more countries, states, and municipalities that are acting. This book is not the place for a comprehensive review of data legislation, but as you can see, change is happening on multiple fronts. That is good, but we need more action.

4.9   *Final thoughts*

In this chapter we reviewed the state of trust in our institutions that are most commonly thought of as engaged in the creation and management of our data. We discussed business in general, business leadership, media companies, and governments.

The overall level of trust granted these organizations by the general public is at an all-time low. These organizations are actively perpetuating a system that is the source of significant and valuable raw material, the users. We do not tolerate companies that egregiously exploit natural resources for the gain of a few. We should not tolerate the same abuse of our data going forward.

We skimmed the surface of legislative and regulatory efforts from governments in Europe, Australia, and the United States relating to our data. Some of the efforts, like those in the EU, are laudable and are having a substantial positive effect on a global basis. Others, like those in the US, are not so effective, and some efforts are not moving in the right direction. This needs to change.

I am optimistic about what can be done, given what has been done in the past six years. The EU governments have shown the way and are leading the way forward. We need to align with these efforts and help shape and provide momentum to this work and these changes.

In the next chapter we'll turn our attention to a topic that has received a serious amount of government attention, press coverage, pundit discussion, and more over the past 30 years: privacy.

Summary

- We need to be aware of the actions and activities by companies, groups, and individuals who have a vested interest in maintaining the status quo regarding our relationship with our data. Many say that they are working in our best interests, but many are not.
- As the new data ecosystem is being defined and built, we need to be aware of the level of trust people feel in relation to companies in general, and specifically in relation to technology companies and media companies.
- New and existing laws from the EU, such as the GDPR, the Data Act, and the Data Governance Act, are defining the new data ecosystem and will shape our relationship with companies and our data.
- Efforts by Australian regulators are of significance and should be noted for their effect on making global technology companies pay for local content and making those companies work collaboratively with local firms.
- US national and state level laws are being written and passed with regularity and will have a significant effect on the ability of US citizens to protect, manage, and monetize their data.

5
Privacy

If the human brain were so simple that we could understand it, we would be so simple that we couldn't.[1]

—IBM research engineer Emerson Pugh

---

[1] Garson O'Toole, "If the human brain were so simple that we could understand it, we would be so simple that we couldn't," *Quote Investigator*, https://quoteinvestigator.com/2016/03/05/brain/.

Privacy has been a charged topic going back to ancient Greece. The US was the first country to expand Constitutional protection to citizen privacy in Supreme Court decisions under the first five and the 14th amendments.[2] Privacy is a very personal topic for most people, evoking strong emotions and feelings.

Privacy means different things to each person. The sphere of data, behavior, and public/private activities where people want or need privacy are unique to each individual. Privacy is especially personal when you consider the types of behavior that people want the most privacy for; we can all understand why there are differences of opinions regarding privacy and closely related topics.

In the minds of many, data ownership and privacy are the same. This is not true. The foundations of data privacy stem from the rights and rules related to data ownership. Given that our views on data ownership as a nation, a society, and as a global population which spans multiple nations are being formed and modified now, it is not surprising that our rules, norms, thoughts, and laws relating to privacy are currently in flux, development, and refinement.

As should be pretty clear by now, this chapter will examine the topic of privacy. Let's start our discussion by defining the term and subject area.

5.1   *Privacy defined*

In the Merriam-Webster's dictionary, *privacy* is defined as

> *1 a: the quality or state of being apart from company or observation: SECLUSION*
>   *b: freedom from unauthorized intrusion: one's right to privacy*
>
> *2 a: SECRECY*
>   *b: a private matter: SECRET*
>
> *3: archaic: a place of seclusion*[3]

In Wikipedia, the definition of privacy is "the ability of an individual or group to seclude themselves or information about themselves, and thereby express themselves selectively."[4]

Our discussion centers on data, and, in today's world, data infers online actions and activity. Winston & Strawn, an international law firm, defines online privacy in this manner: "online privacy is the level of privacy protection an individual has while connected to the Internet. It covers the amount of online security available for personal and financial data, communications, and preferences."[5]

It is intriguing, and somewhat exciting, to examine topics that we think and feel that we know and possibly understand, yet in actuality have spent little time actually thinking about. Privacy, however, is not a simple issue. It is a multifaceted, amorphous

---

[2] Doug Linder, "The Right of Privacy," *Exploring Constitutional Law*, 2021, http://law2.umkc.edu/faculty/projects/ftrials/conlaw/rightofprivacy.html.

[3] "Privacy," *Merriam-Webster*, https://www.merriam-webster.com/dictionary/privacy."

[4] "Privacy," *Wikipedia*, cited on Jan. 16, 2022, https://en.wikipedia.org/wiki/Privacy.

[5] "What is the Definition of Online Privacy?" *Winston & Strawn*, cited on Jan. 16, 2022, https://www.winston.com/en/legal-glossary/online-privacy.html.

topic defined according to societal context, culture, legal framework, time in history, family of origin values, and personal values.

Patricia Brierley Newell suggested in her article "Perspectives on Privacy" that there is no unified and agreed upon definition of privacy. "The nature of privacy is an interesting and complex question which has been addressed in several disciplines. Perspectives on privacy are thus varied, occasionally conflicting, and generally difficult to evaluate in a coherent fashion. There is not, in fact, agreement on what privacy actually is."[6]

Although privacy is something we all take for granted, it is a rarely discussed concept that is far more complex than it first appears. Given the many facets and dimensions of privacy, a discussion of privacy between more than one person can end in confusion and disagreement. We need context to ensure that we are talking about the same shared understanding of privacy to further the dialog and either come to a well understood, shared understanding of the points being discussed, or arrive at a clear point of shared disagreement.

Let's give ourselves a better understanding of privacy throughout time so we can have a deeper and clearer understanding of privacy as it relates to our data, and our actions, in our time.

5.2 *Privacy throughout history*

In Western society, the concept and discussion of private behavior and private property began in ancient Greece, as is the case for many of our foundational laws, norms, and beliefs. The *Stanford Encyclopedia of Philosophy* describes one of the first citations of privacy: "Aristotle's distinction between the public sphere of politics and political activity, the *polis*, and the private or domestic sphere of the family, the *oikos*, as two distinct spheres of life, is a classic reference to a private domain."[7]

"The concept of universal individual privacy is a modern concept primarily associated with Western culture, particularly British and North American cultures, and remained virtually unknown in some cultures until recent times. Now, most cultures recognize the ability of individuals to withhold certain parts of personal information from wider society."[8]

Privacy may be a basic need that reaches beyond humans, but in this book we will limit our discussion and exploration to privacy to data generated by human activities.

5.2.1 *The internet has not eliminated privacy*

A few people, most notably Sun Microsystems CEO Scott McNealy and Meta CEO Mark Zuckerberg, have stated that the advent of modern computing, networking, and social

---

[6] Patricia Brierley Newell, "Perspectives on Privacy," *The Journal of Environmental Psychology*, vol. 15, no. 2 (June 1995): 87–104, http://mng.bz/aM6z.

[7] Judith DeCew, "Privacy," *The Stanford Encyclopedia of Philosophy* (Spring 2018 edition), Edward N. Zalta (ed.), https://plato.stanford.edu/archives/spr2018/entries/privacy/.

[8] "Privacy," *Wikipedia*, cited on Jan. 17, 2022, https://en.wikipedia.org/wiki/Privacy.

media have eliminated privacy as a social norm.[9] We must all beware of individuals and privileged groups making pronouncements that are in their best interests and that are, most likely, not in our best interest in any way at all.

Ann Cavoukian, who was the Information and Privacy Commissioner of the Canadian province of Ontario, remarked in response to the assertion that the norm of privacy had been eliminated by social media: "What I emphatically submit is that there is little evidence to change our view that privacy remains a social norm. Privacy relates to freedom of choice and control in the sphere of one's personal information—choices regarding what information you wish to share and, perhaps more important, what you do not want shared with others. What has changed, however, is the means by which personal information is now readily exchanged, at the speed of light."[10]

Those who will benefit from changing that norm ignore that the only thing that has changed is the external factor created and injected into society (often by them) that makes it seem that "privacy is dead." This is certainly the case with the internet, social media, and the advent of news as entertainment delivered 24 hours a day. The speed, ubiquity, and nature of communications has changed, to be sure, but our basic human need for privacy has not.

5.2.2   *Privacy crosses sociology, psychology, and basic human conditions*

Philosophers and theorists have debated the role of privacy as a basic element of human psychology, and the majority of those leading thinkers have arrived at the conclusion that privacy is a meaningful and valuable concept.

The "Privacy" section of the *Stanford Encyclopedia of Philosophy Archive* contains a compendium of contemporary research supporting the assertion that privacy is an elemental aspect of humans' psychology and sense of well-being:

> *Philosophical debates concerning definitions of privacy became prominent in the second half of the twentieth century, and are deeply affected by the development of privacy protection in the law. Some defend privacy as focusing on control over information about oneself (Parent, 1983), while others defend it as a broader concept required for human dignity (Bloustein, 1964), or crucial for intimacy (Gerstein, 1978; Inness, 1992). Other commentators defend privacy as necessary for the development of varied and meaningful interpersonal relationships (Fried, 1970; Rachels, 1975), or as the value that accords us the ability to control the access others have to us (Gavison, 1980; Allen, 1988; Moore, 2003), or as a set of norms necessary not only to control access but also to enhance personal expression and choice (Schoeman, 1992), or some combination of these (DeCew, 1997). Discussion of the concept is complicated by the fact that privacy appears to be something we value to provide a sphere within which we can be free from interference by others, and yet it also appears to function negatively, as the cloak under which one can hide domination, degradation, or physical harm to women and others.[11]*

[9] Helen A.S. Popkin, "Privacy is dead on Facebook. Get over it." *NBC News*, Jan. 13, 2010, https://www.nbcnews.com/id/wbna34825225.

[10]Ann Cavoukian, "Privacy is still a social norm," *The Globe and Mail*, Mar. 12, 2010, http://mng.bz/eJ4z.

[11]Judith DeCew, "Privacy," *The Stanford Encyclopedia of Philosophy* (Spring 2018 edition), Edward N. Zalta (ed.), https://plato.stanford.edu/archives/spr2018/entries/privacy/.

Privacy is central to human psychology and to a sense of well-being, so much so that it is difficult for many to see the need for privacy, given that it is so interwoven with the core of each individual's sense of self.

5.2.3 *The need for privacy compared to the right of privacy*

The need for privacy has been with humans and animals for centuries. The right to privacy is a more recent invention.

The earliest mention of the right to privacy can be traced back to the *Decretum Gratiani* in Bologna, Italy in the twelfth century, "The concept of a human 'right to privacy' begins when the Latin word *ius* expanded from meaning 'what is fair' to include 'a right—an entitlement a person possesses to control or claim something.'"[12]

I was surprised when researching privacy that the writing, legislation, regulation, and academic dialogue relating to privacy started to accelerate in pace and intensity in the mid to late 1960s. Before 1966, the pace of progress was painfully slow.

James Griffin, explains in his article, "The Human Right to Privacy," published in the *San Diego Law Review*, that in the US, "The U.S. Constitution came into effect in 1789. While not explicitly guaranteeing the right to privacy, the Supreme Court has found that the Constitution does provide for a right to privacy in its First, Third, Fourth, and Fifth amendments."[13]

In the United States, an article in the December 15, 1890, issue of the *Harvard Law Review*, written by attorney Samuel D. Warren and future U.S. Supreme Court Justice Louis Brandeis, entitled "The Right to Privacy," is often cited as the first explicit finding of a US right to privacy. Warren and Brandeis wrote, "that privacy is the right to be let alone and focused on protecting individuals. This approach was a response to recent technological developments of the time, such as photography and sensationalist journalism."[14]

The United Nations Declaration of Human Rights (UDHR) 1948, Article 12 states, "No one shall be subjected to arbitrary interference with his privacy, family, home or correspondence, nor to attacks upon his honor and reputation. Everyone has the right to the protection of the law against such interference or attacks."[15] Today, 122 countries have enacted and enforced privacy laws,[16] although some of those laws are very weak or are not enforced with much rigor.

Think about the activities where you seek privacy, and about the motivating factors for why you seek it. Now overlay those activities with your online activities.

---

[12]"Right to privacy," Wikipedia, cited on Jan. 20, 2022, https://en.wikipedia.org/wiki/Right_to_privacy.

[13]James Griffin, "The Human Right to Privacy" (PDF), *San Diego Law Review*, 2007, p. 3. Retrieved 29 Sept. 2020, cited on Jan. 20, 2022, https://digital.sandiego.edu/sdlr/vol44/iss4/3/.

[14]"Right to privacy," Wikipedia, cited on Jan. 20, 2022, https://en.wikipedia.org/wiki/Right_to_privacy.

[15]"What is Privacy?" *Privacy International*, Oct. 23, 2017, https://privacyinternational.org/explainer/56/what-privacy.

[16]"Data Privacy Laws by Country," *World Population Review*, https://worldpopulationreview.com/country-rankings/data-privacy-laws-by-country.

- Where is the intersection of your desire for privacy and your online activities?
- Would you want more control to access, modify, or delete data related to those activities?
- Would you want to charge companies more money to access your data related to those activities, or would you prefer to block all companies from accessing that data?

Now that we have a more complete mental framework for thinking about and building our broader base of views, beliefs, and feelings about privacy, let's expand our discussion to bring in the psychological aspects of privacy.

5.3   *Psychology and privacy*

As noted earlier, the topic of privacy received sporadic attention for centuries, but in the mid to late 1960s, the topic began to gain attention from a number of diverse fields and areas of interest.

Alan F. Westin, in his 1967 book, *Privacy and Freedom,*[17] "proposes that people need privacy. Privacy, in concert with other needs, helps us to adjust emotionally to day-to-day interpersonal interactions."[18] Westin was a lawyer and a political scientist who examined privacy in relation to the law and personal and organizational behavioral dynamics. "For Westin, privacy was both a dynamic process (i.e., over time, we regulate privacy so it is sufficient for serving momentary needs and role requirements) and a non-monotonic function (i.e., people can have too little, sufficient, or too much privacy)."[19]

In 1975, Irwin Altman, a social psychologist, approached the topic of privacy from a behavioral perspective and presented an analysis of the concept of privacy relating to crowding, territory, and personal space in his book *The Environment and Social Behavior.*

In 2011, Stephen Margulis, a professor at Grand Valley State University, stated that "we continuously adapt our level of privacy and disclosure to internal and external states because we simultaneously need to be open and social as well as private and preserve our autonomy."[20]

In reality, people dynamically calibrate and calculate their needs, wants, and desires in relation to sharing and withholding information moment by moment. All of our relationships have an element of privacy included in the reasoning we are applying and the resulting actions we take and behaviors we exhibit. It's rather surprising that it took until the mid-1960s for privacy to become a prominent topic of research, discussion, and examination.

The consensus that has developed and evolved between and among lawyers, political scientists, sociologists, psychologists, economists, and other theoreticians and

---

[17]Alan F. Westin, *Privacy and Freedom* (New York: Athenum, 1967), pp. xvi, 487.

[18]Stephen T. Margulis, "Three Theories of Privacy: An Overview," chapter 2 in *Privacy Online, Perspectives on Privacy and Self Disclosure on the Social Web*, ed., Sabine Trepte and Leonard Reinecke, pp. 9–17, http://mng.bz/pdGG.

[19]Ibid.

[20]Ibid

practitioners is that privacy is a deep-seated psychological need for humans. The amount of literature and research that has been produced on the topic of privacy in the past 50 years is impressive. Given that so many diverse fields and experts have arrived at similar positions relating to the foundational human need for privacy, it appears that we have arrived at a solid understanding of privacy.

As we are discussing the new and rapidly evolving data ecosystem that we will all be living in, I believe it is important to understand the relevant elements of human psychology and behavior that will come into play within our own minds and the minds of others. If we are aware of the broader and deeper landscape, we can make proactive decisions for ourselves and our families that will provide for greater safety, security, and monetary returns in relation to how we manage and protect our data.

5.4   We need privacy like we need sleep

In the research, theories, and underpinning of the need for privacy, it appears that privacy exhibits many of the characteristics of sleep. Sleep is when our brain undergoes a number of active processes that contribute to the "ability to adapt to input, processing memories, and removal of waste products. When people do not sleep or get enough sleep, symptoms of depression, seizures, high blood pressure and migraines worsen, and immunity is compromised."[21]

Recent studies demonstrate the effect technologies have on how people process and maintain their well-being.[22] Privacy is a mechanism that we all use to maintain mental health and a balanced mental state.

Not everyone has access to the right to privacy, but we all need privacy. In the cases where human rights are restricted or prohibited, people will find a way to meet their basic needs. Secrecy becomes a tool where privacy is not available, so let's expand our discussion to bring in the related topic of secrecy.

5.5   Privacy and secrecy

Privacy and secrecy are often confused. Carol Warren and Barbara Laslett remark in their article "Privacy and Secrecy: A Conceptual Comparison," "Privacy and secrecy both involve boundaries and the denial of access to others; however, they differ in the moral content of the behavior which is concealed. Privacy is consensual where secrecy is not; that is, there is a 'right to privacy' but no equivalent 'right to secrecy.' Those stigmatized or disadvantaged social groups who have little or no access to privacy utilize secrecy to conceal their behavior."[23]

---

[21]"The Science of Sleep: Understanding What Happens When You Sleep," Johns Hopkins Medicine, cited Jan. 23, 2022, https://www.hopkinsmedicine.org/health/wellness-and-prevention/
the-science-of-sleep-understanding-what-happens-when-you-sleep.

[22]"The Social Dilemma: Social Media and Your Mental Health," *McLean Hospital*, Dec. 2, 2022, https://www.mcleanhospital.org/essential/it-or-not-social-medias-affecting-your-mental-health.

[23]Carol Warren and Barbara Laslett, "Privacy and Secrecy: A Conceptual Comparison," *Journal of Social Issues*, Summer 1977, http://mng.bz/Opyn.

It is an interesting concept and premise that people who are not granted, or those who do not have access to, the right of privacy, due to being deprived of privacy by an organization or government or other oppressive force, resort to secrecy to protect themselves and their well-being and possibly their lives. It is a subtle difference, but it has a dramatic effect on human safety, mental well-being, and psychological safety. When people know they are deprived of the right of privacy, they will feel anxious, nervous, and worried about concealing data and information that may disadvantage them or their loved ones, colleagues, or compatriots.

When people know that the government, a business, or other organization is enacting and enforcing surveillance, they will suffer. They will change their behavior, and these changes propagate through all aspects of the personal and professional lives of the people subject to the surveillance. Stephen T. Margulis explains in his article "Privacy as a Social Issue and Behavioral Concept," "Losses of privacy have the potential for life-and-death costs when a person has as a critical goal the concealment of his or her intentions (e.g., moles and double agents; Richelson, 1995) or identity. For example, during World War II, Stevens (2001), a Jewish male, passing as Christian, worked for the Nazis during the day and served in an anti-Semitic, anti-Nazi Polish underground group at night."[24]

In most cases, secrecy is employed as a last resort and is done so under conditions of stress and fear. While in casual contemplation, it is easy to conflate privacy and secrecy, but once you actively examine the two topics, you can understand and internalize that people need to be assured that they have a right to privacy and that this right is recognized, granted, and protected.

5.6   *Two sides of privacy*

Privacy can be used in a positive or negative manner, as often seems the case with foundational beliefs, elements of human behavior, and rights that all humans consider essential or at least very important.

As research illustrates, privacy, when employed in an ethical and transparent manner, provides for a sense of well-being, relief, and comfort, and it contributes to balanced mental health. Privacy enables people to withdraw information or their physical self from the public view. There they can process private thoughts and feelings, enabling them to be grounded and happy. They can know they have taken care to protect themselves, their loved ones, friends, and associates from harms, real or perceived. This is the light side of privacy. Of course, there is a dark side of privacy.

The dark side of privacy is often discussed in relation to strong data encryption. An example of strong encryption being used on a daily basis is in encrypted messaging services such as Telegram, Signal, Threema, WhatsApp, and others.[25] Strong encryption

---

[24]Stephen T. Margulis, "Privacy as a Social Issue and Behavioral Concept," *Journal of Social Issues*, vol. 59, no. 2 (2003), pp. 243–261, https://www.sfu.ca/~palys/Margulis-2003-PrivacyAsASocialIssue&BehavioralConcept.pdf.

[25]John Corpuz, "The best encrypted messaging apps in 2022," Jan. 23, 2022, cited Jan. 26, 2022, *Tom's Guide*, https://www.tomsguide.com/reference/best-encrypted-messaging-apps.

enables people to communicate in a manner that is untraceable, unreadable, and that cannot be accessed by most external parties. Encrypted messaging ensures that monitoring of communications for the purposes of government surveillance, corporate espionage, or other nefarious purposes cannot be enacted in the majority of cases. A subset of people, groups, and governments also use these applications and encryption for unethical, immoral, or illegal activities. This state of affairs poses a problem for governmental and legal authorities and people or companies, and for communities that these groups may seek to undermine or harm.

Some of the more dubious uses of privacy are outlined by Stephen T. Margulis in his article "Privacy as a Social Issue and Behavioral Concept," such as "misuse of a public office (Westin, 1967) and vandalism (Altman, 1975), and morally dubious behavior like lying (Derlega & Chaikin, 1977). For example, DePaulo, Wetzel, Sternglanz & Walker Wilson . . . make a strong case for how claims to privacy can provide the latitude to deceive others. They argue that everyday deceptions are aided by our tendency to honor claims others make about themselves but that our tendency also enables less scrupulous individuals to use deception to exploit others."[26]

Privacy and secrecy have been used in positive and negative manners throughout human history. Where privacy is employed, there is an opportunity for the darker side of human behavior to take hold and influence how people act. We have seen this recently in the move toward authoritarian governments and the actions of technology and media companies.

When privacy is employed to protect our data, information, actions, and good intentions of people, it can be a powerful force for good and positive change. The opposite can also be true and poses a serious conundrum for parties on both sides of charged and contentious issues.

5.7 Privacy and human behavior

Privacy is such an intriguing topic: widely considered important, hotly debated in certain circles such as think tanks, universities, and other temples of highbrow thought, sporadically taken up in the halls of government, and discussed infrequently at the dinner table. People profess that they want a high degree of privacy, but then they regularly act in ways that actively reduce or eliminate the degree of privacy that they actually have. It is a paradox, but there are numerous paradoxes in human behavior; that is one of the reasons that life is so remarkably interesting.

Mary Madden and Lee Rainie, from the Pew Research Center, outline their findings about the paradox we see in people's behavior in their article "Americans' Attitudes About Privacy, Security and Surveillance":

> *Most Americans hold strong views about the importance of privacy in their everyday lives. The majority of Americans believe it is important—often "very important"—that they be able to maintain privacy and confidentiality in commonplace activities of their lives. Most*

---

[26]Stephen T. Margulis, "Privacy as a Social Issue and Behavioral Concept," *Journal of Social Issues*, vol. 59, no. 2 (2003), pp. 243–261, https://www.sfu.ca/~palys/Margulis-2003-PrivacyAsASocialIssue&BehavioralConcept.pdf.

strikingly, these views are especially pronounced when it comes to knowing what information about them is being collected and who is doing the collecting. These feelings also extend to their wishes that they be able to maintain privacy in their homes, at work, during social gatherings, at times when they want to be alone and when they are moving around in public.

When they are asked to think about all of their daily interactions—both online and offline— and the extent to which certain privacy-related values are important to them, clear majorities say these dimensions are at least "somewhat important" and many express the view that these aspects of personal information control are "very important."

Survey results from early 2015 show:

- *93% of adults say that being in control of who can get information about them is important; 74% feel this is "very important," while 19% say it is "somewhat important."*
- *90% say that controlling what information is collected about them is important— 65% think it is "very important" and 25% say it is "somewhat important."*

At the same time, Americans also value having the ability to share confidential matters with another trusted person. Nine-in-ten (93%) adults say this ability is important to them, with 72% saying it is "very important" and 21% saying it is "somewhat important."[27]

It is clear that people want and need to actively manage their privacy and ability to withhold selected information from entities they don't trust (e.g., the government) but share the same information with those they do trust. Given the fluid nature of online activities, the changing behaviors of people and the evolving norms and expectations of society, it is not surprising that, today, people find navigating and maintaining a solid understanding of their privacy preferences and needs difficult and confusing.

Privacy is clearly desired by the vast majority of people, but many of those same people are not aware of the principles and foundations of privacy in relation to their needs and wants for it.

5.8   *Privacy precepts*

We are now aware of the definition of privacy. We know the importance of the need for privacy, and what the right to privacy is. We have compared and contrasted privacy to related concepts like secrecy. But what are the conditions or foundational elements that are needed before the right to privacy can exist and operate in a societal context?

Microsoft's privacy statement and policy is 11 pages long and 3,371 words.[28] The primary purpose of the Microsoft privacy statement and policy is not to inform individuals of how Microsoft is collecting, using, and leveraging your data of all types; it is to protect Microsoft from you exercising your rights related to your data.

Figure 5.1 presents the principles of privacy from the University of Michigan.

---

[27]Mary Madden and Lee Rainie, "Americans' Attitudes About Privacy, Security and Surveillance," Pew Research Center, May 20, 2015,, https://www.pewresearch.org/internet/2015/05/20/americans-attitudes-about-privacy-security-and-surveillance/.

[28]"Microsoft Privacy Statement," *Microsoft*, Last updated Dec. 2021, cited Jan. 27, 2022, https://privacy.microsoft .com/en-us/privacystatement.

Privacy at U-M

When it comes to privacy, we are guided by the following principles:

Respect
Valuing U-M community members' right to privacy and striving to be the leaders and best in the ways we manage and protect personal information

Transparency
Creating visibility to our data collection, usage, and sharing practices

Accountability
Taking responsibility for the ethical and secure handling of your personal information

Knowledge
Creating, curating, and disseminating information and resources to grow privacy awareness across the U-M community and beyond

Empowerment
As appropriate, providing actionable information on how to protect your and others' privacy

Figure 5.1   Privacy at University of Michigan[29]

This is the first sentence from the Dell privacy statement: "Your privacy is important to us, and our commitment to core privacy values of transparency, control, respect and trust."[30] Microsoft, the University of Michigan, and Dell have extensive privacy policies, but in contrast to Microsoft, the other two are written so the majority of people can read and understand them. The statements preceding the privacy policies of Dell and the University of Michigan act as a preamble and spell out the foundational principles of privacy that these organizations are offering to each of us in plain, simple, clear language.

Not many people search out and read the privacy statements and policies of the companies they interact with. The content of those statements tell a great deal about the orientation and view of those companies in relation to your data and your privacy. Then you can make a decision as to whether you want those companies to collect, store, and leverage your data.

Let's move the focus of our discussion from foundational precepts and concepts to commercial companies and their privacy statements and policies. Partially due to the GDPR, almost all companies have a privacy policy posted on their website. Let's examine those statements and policies to see what they really say and who they protect.

---

[29]"Privacy at U-M," Information and Technology Services, Safe Computing, University of Michigan, , cited Jan. 20, 2022, https://safecomputing.umich.edu/privacy/privacy-u-m.

[30]"Privacy Statement Regarding Customer and Online User Information," *Dell*, cited on Jan. 27, 2022, https://www.dell.com/learn/us/en/uscorp1/policies-privacy.

5.9   Poor privacy policies

In reading a privacy policy from a healthcare provider, I learned that this healthcare provider will share your most protected data, personal health information (PHI), with nearly every organization that they have ever done business with, even in a tangential manner:

> Health care providers including, but not limited to doctors, nurses, X-ray technicians, pharmacists, administrative personnel in various offices, lab technicians, dentists, dental assistants, dental hygienists, nursing homes staff, senior living facilities staff, memory care facilities staff. And . . .

> Third party payors such as insurance companies, governmental agencies, health plan operators, collection agencies, consulting firms working on operational analyses, students, trainees, firms that are contracted to develop training for staff, regulatory bodies and consulting organizations tasked with assessing the quality of care provided, external bodies that are responsible for certifying residence operations and staff, service providers involved in the provision of care such as lawyers, accountants, and others, organizations that assist in developing strategic and tactical plans for future expansion and operations, arbitration professionals, other firms that may want to buy the operations or firms that may want to merge operations, organizations that may provide services to analyze the cost of operations, firms that consult on de-identifying data. And . . .

I like this list the best:

> Any health care provider that has had a relationship with you at any time in your life, guardians, conservators, family members, close friends, providers of emergency services, public health authorities, people authorized by public health authorities, the Federal Food and Drug Administration (FDA), local, state, and federal agencies responsible for investigating abuse, health oversight agencies, law enforcement personnel, coroners, medical examiners, funeral directors, researchers, organ and tissue donation organizations, military personnel, veterans affairs personnel, military command authorities, national security and intelligence personnel, presidential protective services personnel, the US Department of Health and Human Services, worker's compensation personnel.

Why does the Secret Service for the President of the United States of America need your health data? Your PHI data can be shared with anyone, and this is the data that has the *most* protection in the United States. Who is not on these lists? It might have been a shorter list to say who they would not share your PHI data with.

If this is the level of protection afforded to us regarding our most protected data, it is clear that protecting your privacy and your data is not in the best interests of the companies that you are engaging with. As it is up to you to protect your data, it is up to you to manage your privacy.

5.10   Enlightened privacy policies and related data protection

Some organizations have a more enlightened view of data and how privacy will need to evolve. Many of those organizations are in Europe. There are significant and serious discussions about how the lack of privacy is hindering valuable data sharing that can be used to improve health care and the development of new drugs and therapies.

Professor Mark Lawler, scientific director at the DATA-CAN health data research hub and professor of digital health at Queen's University Belfast remarked, "If the increased sharing of health data is to become a key factor in improving healthcare and the lives of patients around the globe, privacy security will need to develop just as quickly. This doesn't just mean complying with regulations set out by the General Data Protection Regulation (GDPR) or the US Health Insurance Portability and Accountability Act (HIPAA). It also means encrypting data and restricting access to it, as well as educating the staff that work within the healthcare system and handle sensitive data."[31]

Professor Lawler went on to say, "'Rather than data moving around and running the risk of potential privacy breaches, you keep the data in a very safe environment and then you have safe researchers who are trained to deal with privacy issues,' he explains. 'We sometimes call it the five safes; safe people working in safe environments with safe technology looking at developing safe outputs that are relevant to patients' leading to safe data."[32]

Governments around the world are debating, discussing, and formulating more effective laws to ensure that privacy is provided and maintained in a manner that is driven by the interests of individuals. For now, we, as individuals, need to be vigilant about who we provide our data to and how we protect our data and our privacy.

5.11 Privacy laws and regulations

Alan Westin was a Professor of Public Law and Government at Columbia University. His research in the 1960s is widely seen as the first significant work on the problem of consumer privacy and data protection. His 1967 book *Privacy and Freedom* was a pioneering work that prompted US privacy legislation and helped launch global privacy movements in many democratic nations in the 1960s and 1970s.[33]

National governments around the world have recognized the need for privacy legislation. This movement has been driven primarily by the demands of their constituents. People around the world want more control over their data and their privacy. As of November 2021, 128 out of 194 countries had put in place legislation to secure the protection of data and privacy.[34]

The United States has numerous federal laws relating to privacy, and individual US states have been very active in formulating, debating, evolving, rejecting, and passing privacy laws. In 2021, "13 states… enacted 17 consumer data privacy bills and two states adopted resolutions providing for studies on the issue. Comprehensive privacy legislation was introduced in at least 25 states, and two states, Colorado, and Virginia, followed California by enacting comprehensive consumer data privacy legislation."[35]

---

[31]Alice Broster, "Why data privacy is crucial to the future of healthcare," *Raconteur*, Jan. 19, 2022, http://mng.bz/Y60N.

[32]Ibid.

[33]Alan F. Westin, *Privacy and Freedom* (New York: Athenum, 1967), pp. xvi, 487.

[34]"Data Protection and Privacy Legislation Worldwide," *United Nations Conference on Trade and Development*, cited Jan. 28, 2022, https://unctad.org/page/data-protection-and-privacy-legislation-worldwide.

[35]"2021 Consumer Data Privacy Legislation," *National Conference of State Legislatures*, Dec. 27, 2021, cited on Jan. 28, 2022, https://www.ncsl.org/research/telecommunications-and-information-technology/2021-consumer-data-privacy-legislation.aspx.

Figure 5.2   Data protection and privacy legislation worldwide[36]

This is a fast-moving area of legislation, and by the time you read this book there will be more and newer privacy statutes on the books and in force. For the current list of legislation that has been passed, rejected, and current laws that are under development, refer to the National Conference of State Legislatures site.[37]

National and state governments are working on a wide range of laws to provide more privacy protections for individuals to give each of us more access and control over the data all organizations collect from us. It will take time, but the laws are in the works. It is important to keep in mind that the entire concept of data, data ownership, and privacy is in flux and development. The laws in process will have to be augmented, revised, repealed, and replaced in the near future as the concept of data ownership is changed.

As we discussed in chapter 3, once the concept of data ownership is defined in the traditional sense to reflect our ownership of our data, the concept of privacy and law as relating to privacy will change again.

5.12   *Privacy and data ownership*

Many of the current views, policies, statements, and laws related to privacy are based on the premise that the data in question, our data, is actually owned by the companies that recorded it. This is incorrect. When one of the foundational views, premises, or precepts

[36]Ibid.
[37]Ibid.

used to formulate a position, law, or opinion is incorrect, then the resulting concept will be incorrect as well. This is part of the reason why the law is ever changing.

As the common understanding of the true ownership of data evolves to where a significant minority of the people know that their data is truly owned by them, they will demand that privacy statements, privacy policies, laws, and related regulations change to reflect this new reality. Privacy-related laws, regulations, and data sharing agreements are all improving the amount of privacy we have without requiring us to change our current behaviors. There will be even more change in the coming years. Once the issue of data ownership is corrected and legislated, the issue of privacy will come to the forefront of change.

5.13   *Privacy and technology*

When you access a website via Google's Chrome browser, do you use the incognito mode? In the perception of a number of users, this feature indicates that your browsing activity will not be tracked while using Chrome. Go to the settings in Chrome and select New Incognito Window (Ctrl-Shift-N) and the resulting browser window will look like figure 5.3.

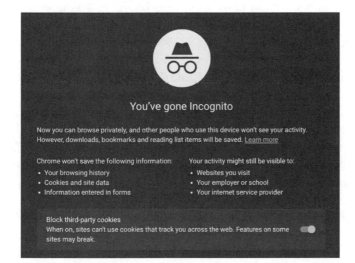

Figure 5.3   Setting incognito mode in Chrome

It is clear to technology savvy people that you are really not gaining any protection by using the Incognito function. Your activity is not logged to the local computer, but the sites you visit, the traffic you generate, and the data created and shared is still logged in all the places we discussed in chapter 2.

Technology companies want the public to believe that they are working to provide options that will enable people to increase their privacy and let them have a bit more control over their data. For the most part, though, these efforts to date have been more obfuscation than real functionality and true progress in making privacy a reality that's within reach of all users.

In late 2021, Sarah Krouse reported in her article "Google CEO Pichai Can Face Questions in 'Incognito Mode' Suit, Judge Rules" that there was cause to believe that Google had misled users into believing that the incognito mode provided more privacy to users than it actually does. "Plaintiffs in a California court case alleging Google illegally tracked consumers when they used 'incognito mode' in its Chrome web browser can question Alphabet CEO Sundar Pichai, a federal judge ruled. The suit filed in 2020 by three users seeking $5 billion says Google invaded consumers' privacy by collecting information about their browsing despite their use of the private mode. Google has said its privacy policy states that using 'incognito mode' does not stop all tracking, it just means your activity is not saved on the browser or device."[38]

One of the more recent efforts by Facebook to put a new face on their rampant misuse of data is a department named Facebook Civic Integrity team. A former Facebook employee remarked, "My coworkers and I researched and fixed integrity problems—abuses of the platform to spread hoaxes, hate speech, harassment, calls to violence, and so on. Over time, we became experts, thanks to all the people, hours, and data thrown at the problem."[39] There is little evidence of this actually happening. Facebook is a massive content management system and advertising machine driven by algorithms and a profit maximization objective on overdrive. Any person who thinks that human intervention has a chance of turning the tide of trampling privacy, misusing data, and reducing the incitement to hate and violence is living in a fantasy.

Mobile apps suffer the same shortcomings. Users can fiddle with the settings to reduce the amount of data logged and stored by the app provider, but you will have little to no luck in significantly reducing the amount of data that the companies hoard. Technology and online media companies have too much to gain to self-regulate. You have learned this by now. To regain our privacy and control of our data, we need to have the government step in.

Beyond technology companies, technologies themselves are playing a part in the steady march of eroding our privacy. People are concerned that AI will foster a loss of privacy. Jason Corso, Brinning Professor of Computer Science and Director of Stevens Institute for Artificial Intelligence at Stevens Institute of Technology, published a recent report titled, "A Perspective on Americans' Attitudes Toward Artificial Intelligence." He found that "Loss of privacy tops the list of concerns about the negative consequences of AI, with three in four adults voicing that concern. However, age affects those opinions: among generations, GenZers are least concerned (62%), while Baby Boomers are most concerned (80%)."[40]

---

[38]Sarah Krouse, "Google CEO Pichai Can Face Questions in 'Incognito Mode' Suit, Judge Rules," *The Information,* Dec. 29, 2021, https://www.theinformation.com/briefings/google-ceo-pichai-can-face-questions-in-incognito-mode-suit-judge-rules.

[39]Sahar Massachi, "How to save our social media by treating it like a city," MIT Technology Review, Dec. 20, 2021, https://www.technologyreview.com/2021/12/20/1042709/how-to-save-social-media-treat-it-like-a-city/.

[40]Jason Corso, "A Perspective on Americans' Attitudes Toward Artificial Intelligence," *Stevens TechPulse Report,* Nov. 15, 2021, https://www.stevens.edu/news/stevens-techpulse-report.

5.14 Privacy and trust

We spent the entire chapter 4 examining trust, but the intersection of privacy and trust are worth a few moments of our time and attention. The need for privacy is an innate part of all humans. Trust is a "belief that someone or something is reliable, good, honest, effective, etc."[41] Both privacy and trust are ephemeral and can be harmed in a moment with a dishonest action or by a pattern of deceptive behavior.

Nothing in the world of data can diminish our need and desire for privacy. But governments, universities, companies, and people are working on providing the foundations for the right to privacy, which is encouraging. Our trust in governments, companies, our educational systems, and each other has been severely tested. Even though some organizations and individuals have tried and are trying to completely destroy our trust, they have not been successful. They have driven many people to despair, resignation, and rage, but they have not extinguished the belief in and efforts to restore trust in our systems, interactions, and societies.

It is hard to see a day when ubiquitous trust is restored, but I do believe that we will build the legal, ethical, and community-based frameworks needed for us to have trust between individuals and governments, companies, and all levels of our educational systems.

5.15 Final thoughts

Privacy is a topic that we think we know about, but when we delve into it, we find that we only have high-level perceptions and vague notions conceived from the tidbits of information we have blithely and casually consumed over our lifetimes. Even the delineation of the need for and the right to privacy are not fully defined in the minds of most people. As we discussed, the need for privacy is innate in humans, but the right to privacy has only been seriously examined, researched, and discussed since 1966.

It is surprising how long it takes for a topic to move from discovery and research to common knowledge. While examining the topic of data science for my previous book, I learned that accounting had been with society for centuries. It is widely understood and taught in universities and it is ubiquitous in all companies around the world, but data science and analytics as a subject has been with us for 80 years and only now is the subject beginning to be taught at the university level.

When we think about where we have encountered information about privacy, some has come from the news, and other pieces have come from casual conversation, but we can almost be assured that relatively little or none came to us during our educational experiences.

Given that privacy has been a recognized and seriously researched topic for less than 60 years, it will take a few more decades for the subject to become ingrained in the educational systems and society at large and therefore become common knowledge.

---

[41]"Trust," *Merriam-Webster,* https://www.merriam-webster.com/dictionary/trust.

We must be aware that most of the information we hold about privacy comes from sources that contain a significant amount of inherent bias.

Privacy has aspects that intersect with numerous behaviors and beliefs. Once those elements are brought together, the tapestry of the related concepts begin to flow together in an intriguing view of the concept of human behavior. Furthermore, our own behaviors and reactions are seen in a new and perhaps surprising light. When these foundational elements of our beliefs, needs, rights, fears, and experiences are examined, we then see that some of our behaviors are actually working against our own good and the good of our families, communities, and societies.

Our data is more powerful than most people know. Our need for privacy and desire for trust are elemental driving forces. Most people do not spend time contemplating the elemental driving forces of the human psyche; I suppose that is the work of philosophers and academics, for the most part. But when there are actors and actions actively working against our foundational beliefs, rights, and needs, we must step back and course-correct for our well-being, that of our families, and of society as a whole.

Our privacy, trust, and data are worth our attention and action. We can make a difference in how all of them are fostered, nurtured, and cared for. We just have to pay attention and act, and it is time to act.

Summary

- Privacy is a basic human need and a foundational behavioral element.
- Privacy extends beyond humans to other animals as well.
- Privacy is as old as the human race, but only recently has the topic received significant and serious examination, research, and study.
- The intersection of privacy with the related topics of secrecy, trust, data ownership, human psychology, and technology provide an interesting lens through which to examine and understand the new data ecosystem that is being built today.

Moving from Open Data to Our Data

This chapter covers

- Moving from data as a closed monopoly controlled by companies to an open ecosystem controlled by individuals

- The laws in place and legislation in process to govern and enable active control and management of data by groups and individuals

- New organizations to manage Open Data/Our Data, including data pools, data commons, and data exchanges

- The creation of data intermediaries as an interface for individuals to manage Our Data

This is not my beautiful house. This is not my beautiful wife. Well, how did I get here?[1]

—David Byrne

---

[1] David Byrne, "Once in a Lifetime," *Ride, Rise Roar*, 2010, cited Jan. 30, 2022, http://davidbyrne.com/explore/ride-rise-roar/explore.

We have been discussing several historical and current contextual elements that surround data, including legal and psychological issues, corporate misuse, and ill-defined ownership. At this point in the book, you may despair at the scale of the problem, but hang in there. Change is coming, and sooner than you might think. This chapter may bring some hope.

The creation of Open Data[2] over the past two decades has been a huge success for companies, organizations, and people around the world. Open Data, similar in concept to open source code, makes the government transparent, unlocks the secrets of disease, creates new drugs, and is crucial to the development of software applications and layers of intelligence that were not possible before Open Data. And while the corporate world has benefited financially from Open Data, it cannot horde it for profit. The development of "Our Data" is the next stage in the evolution of Open Data.[3]

Azeem Azhar advocates for Open Data in his daily newsletter, *Exponential View*. He calls for a power shift from companies to individuals when it comes to accessing, managing, leveraging, and monetizing personal data. "Long-term readers of this newsletter will know of my interest in collective approaches to benefiting from aggregate data. Today's models largely rely on data monopolies stockpiling and exploiting that data. Collective approaches (which are still few and far between) change the balance of power away from centralized aggregators and towards the end users, acting together."[4]

McKinsey and Company, the global consultancy, produced a report in 2021 that predicts that by 2025 organizations will rely on data exchanges and data pooling to increase the value and accuracy of their analytics. In their "The data-driven enterprise of 2025" article for McKinsey, Neil Assur and Kayvaun Rowshankish stated, "Large, complex organizations use data-sharing platforms to facilitate collaboration on data-driven projects, both within and between organizations. Data-driven companies actively participate in a data economy that facilitates the pooling of data to create more valuable insights for all members. Data marketplaces enable the exchange, sharing, and supplementation of data, ultimately empowering companies to build truly unique and proprietary data products and gain insights from them. Altogether, barriers to the exchange and combining of data are greatly reduced, bringing together various data sources in such a way that the value generated is much greater than the sum of its parts."[5]

As Azhar and McKinsey indicate, we are moving from a data ecosystem that is closed, monopolistic, and controlled by companies to an open ecosystem where each individual can play an active, engaged, proactive role in shaping how our data is used.

---

[2] "Open Data Essentials," *The World Bank*, http://opendatatoolkit.worldbank.org/en/essentials.html.

[3] "What is Open Data?" *Open Data Handbook*, https://opendatahandbook.org/guide/en/what-is-open-data/.

[4] Azeem Azhar, "Quantum puzzle; crypto & the mirror of Erised; dark proteome ++ #357," *Exponential View*, Jan 30, 2022, https://www.exponentialview.co/.

[5] Neil Assur and Kayvaun Rowshankish, "The data driven enterprise of 2025," McKinsey & Company, Jan. 28, 2022, https://www.mckinsey.com/business-functions/mckinsey-analytics/our-insights/the-data-driven-enterprise-of-2025.

6.1   *Data from many sources drives value*

Over the past 100 years, organizations on the leading edge of monetizing data have done so by aggregating data. AC Nielsen, IRI, Google, and others started by accumulating and offering the most significant aggregation of a singular data type. You can see this in direct mail companies, Wal-Mart, insurance companies, like Progressive, and others across a diverse range of industries.

We are well past the era of simply aggregating one type of data as the leading driver of value. Today, companies must accumulate and integrate multiple data sources. The analytics business has been doing this with consistently improving results for over 40 years.

To determine the best place to put a facility, from an urgent care clinic to an electric vehicle charging station, you accumulate data for traffic, population, demographics, existing and competing facilities, pricing, employment, and almost anything else related to your market. All these data sets provide a clear picture of the potential locations for building the new facility. In contrast, site selection applications in the past mainly relied on traffic and population density as the primary sources of data. The world of data has become very rich and valuable across all types of applications due to the availability of a wide range of data sources that can be easily obtained, integrated, and analyzed.

The state of the art in data and analytics, while becoming more popular, remains a small industry and is not well known by the general public for a few reasons:

- It is quite nerdy and technical; the vast majority of people would find it dull and not very interesting.
- Only a handful of people know how to do it well and consistently.
- It offers a competitive advantage. Companies would prefer to not talk about it lest their competitors learn of their secrets, systems, and actions.
- When customers hear about this depth of data analysis they are often taken aback.

6.2   *Data and analytics at dinner parties*

When people ask me what I do professionally, I used to say I helped companies turn data into money and then expanded on that statement. I would tell people about actual programs that I, or my teams, had worked on. I would explain how we used data to predict how much money individuals would be willing to pay for services or programs. We would tell companies where they should ship products proactively based on our predictions, such as where to ship beer based on the predicted temperature and weather data. Or I would tell stories about how my teams have created systems that increase the cross-selling and upselling of products when customers called in for customer support.

The responses were mildly to seriously incredulous and predominantly negative. People would say things like, "You can get enough data about me to predict what I am going to do or how companies can make more money from me?" I would say yes, we can, and we do this today. They would say things like, "That is creepy," or "I don't like that," or "How do I stop that from happening?" Rarely would people ask how we did that or what data was needed to do it. They didn't ask, in my opinion, because they were taken off guard or they just didn't care.

Now, at parties and social gatherings (pre-COVID, of course), after the first statement when they want to know more, I just say I help companies and people understand the behavior of partners, customers, competitors, and interested parties. That is innocuous enough that they generally drop the subject, or I ask them a question to redirect the dialogue in a different direction. From my informal testing, it seems that when you bring in the fact that companies and markets are the primary target of the data and analytical work rather than individuals, that is enough to reduce or remove people's discomfort.

6.3   *Data can be used as a weapon*

For the majority of the previous 40 years, data and analytics have evolved into a tailored approach to making money and providing a defensible competitive advantage. The majority of people involved in these activities and the market, either as practitioners or users or consumers of the data and analytics products and services, saw no reason to advertise or communicate what we were doing or why we were doing it.

The industry has grown substantially in the last four decades. It is no longer a secret; the knowledge of to how to aggregate, integrate, and use data for competitive advantage is no longer held by a small number of practicing professionals. To be clear, this is not common knowledge either, but the industry has grown beyond the handful of practitioners who taught me how to perform data and analytics as a craft and a profession.

As an indication of how much the industry has grown, look at the pronouncements and press relating to data and analytics. In 2012, Tom Davenport and D.J. Patil pronounced in an article in the *Harvard Business Review*, "Data Scientist: The Sexiest Job of the 21st Century."[6] This article alone put data and analytics on a completely new trajectory.

People and firms are now routinely weaponizing data and analytics to the detriment of others and the public in general. Companies, special interest groups, political groups, and other organizations are using data and analytics to push ideas, concepts, and narratives that are not true. This cannot be allowed to proliferate.

6.4   *The horse is out of the barn, let's go riding . . .*

When I started in the data and analytics business, we talked about the duty of care that we needed to undertake to ensure that the data and analytics we were working with, and building, were used for commercial, ethical, and value-added purposes. We talked

---

[6] Thomas H. Davenport and D.J. Patil, "Data Scientist: The Sexiest Job of the 21st Century," *Harvard Business Review*, October 2012, https://hbr.org/2012/10/data-scientist-the-sexiest-job-of-the-21st-century.

about, and were concerned with, the possibility of firms using data and analytics to disadvantage others, but that type of activity was rare and frowned upon. And we as practitioners, for the most part, had a code of ethics to guide us in our efforts.[7] The majority of people I worked with were PhDs in psychology and sociology and had a deep understanding of the ethical element of data and analytics.

The people who hired us were primarily interested in commercial gain, and we steered away from unethical uses of data and analytics. However, as the industry has grown, the people who are using the tools, techniques, and technologies have moved into activities that harm individuals, groups, and society.

One of the first projects I executed on my own was for a consumer packaged-goods company. I was asked by a senior manager to examine promotion, pricing, and sales data in the US for two product lines over a number of years. Data had been painstakingly collected on the pricing and promotional programs that were designed and implemented over multiple decades.

I took the data, cleaned and integrated it, and produced the requested analysis. When I presented the findings, my client was surprised, and not in a good way. The analysis illustrated that the programs deployed by this firm, and by many other competitive firms in the US and global market, had conditioned retailers and consumers to wait for and rely on price reductions and other price-related promotions to buy the products. When sales and shipment volumes were analyzed on an equivalent basis over time, it showed the results of these programs over decades was to drive down prices and simultaneously reduce the overall purchasing volume. This was the exact opposite of the stated and desired objective.

After I presented the findings of the analysis to the project sponsor, he asked me to hold off on presenting or talking about the data until he had left the company, which was in three months. It was sad that he felt that way. It wasn't just him as an individual who drove this result, it was the whole of the industry and the overuse of price and promotion in the market in general, but he was embarrassed and surprised by the reality of the situation.

Also, it was unethical of him to direct me to bury the analysis. I worked on the account for nearly two years. I did wait until the agreed-upon time to share the analysis. When I did, no one blamed him for the outcomes. They all knew anecdotally what was happening—the data and analysis only confirmed their tacit knowledge.

We have moved from mildly unethical suppression of data, analytics, and results to provide a single manager cover instead of standing up and accepting responsibility for his decisions, to seriously dangerous and duplicitous intentional use of data to mislead, deceive, and disadvantage people.

Until recently, most data used in data and analytics was based on primary research, transactions, claims, demographics, travel data, and other easily gathered, repetitive data. Today, the sources of data that are available are mind boggling. Governments

---

[7] "Data Science Code of Professional Conduct," *Data Science Association*, https://www.datascienceassn.org/code-of-conduct.html

and companies are offering data of almost unimaginable variety. Not only is it data from real-world activities, it is also data synthetically manufactured to support a false claim, to create conditions that suit a particular aim, or to justify certain actions unsupported by reality. This is not data and analytics. This is deception and deceit.

6.5   *New and modern approaches to data*

We want and need changes in the way that society views data and how the laws relating to data ownership and privacy work and are enforced. Those societal and legal changes are in process and will force change in the way companies collect, manage, and provide us with access to our data.

Elinor Ostrom (née Awan) was born in Los Angeles in 1933 and grew up during the Great Depression. She studied political science at the University of California, Los Angeles, where she received her PhD in 1965. Ostrom won the 2009 Nobel Prize in Economic Sciences for her work on understanding and explaining how common resources are managed in varying governing environments.

Before Ostrom's groundbreaking career, research, collaborations, and market-changing insights, "It was long unanimously held among economists that natural resources that were collectively used by their users would be over-exploited and destroyed in the long-term. Elinor Ostrom disproved this idea by conducting field studies on how people in small, local communities manage shared natural resources, such as pastures, fishing waters, and forests. She showed that when natural resources are jointly used by their users, in time, rules are established for how these are to be cared for and used in a way that is both economically and ecologically sustainable."[8]

In the 1980s, after spending over 15 years studying group dynamics in multiple fields, Ostrom returned to studying common resource pools, but this time with the recognition that the underlying dynamic being studied was that of common pool resource management. Elinor and Vincent Ostrom's research focused on how governmental policies and overlapping, intersecting, and conflicting interests affected the performance of urban police agencies, irrigation systems, and forestry management regimes.[9]

The primary insights that came out of Ostrom's research were that common pools of resources were often managed by groups of interested individuals much more efficiently than similar pools managed by externally organized people groups (i.e., government agencies). Their research illustrated that organically organized groups optimized resources 74% of the time as opposed to 42% of the time for governmental bodies.[10]

Her work created a new understanding of the actual delineation between common resources and private property. She and her colleagues clarified and codified how organically organized groups optimized the management of common resources for

---

[8] "Elinor Ostrom," *The Nobel Prize*, https://www.nobelprize.org/prizes/economic-sciences/2009/ostrom/facts/.
[9] Ibid.
[10] "Elinor Ostrom, Prize Lecture," *The Nobel Prize*, 2009, https://www.nobelprize.org/prizes/economic-sciences/2009/ostrom/lecture/.

long term sustainability in opposition to the previously held theory that all common pool resources would be exploited, depleted, and most likely destroyed.

Her work, and that of her many collaborators, formed a significant portion of the basis for the idea that Open Data and open source software would work and work well for these common resource systems, and she was right. Now these open systems based on her field and theoretical work form the basis for, and are a significant part of, the future of aggregating and sharing data and building systems based on data and software.

From the work of Elinor Ostrom and others, the advocates of Open Data and open software extended her research, findings, and insights from forestry, irrigation, and policing systems to the new worlds of data and software.

6.5.1   *Open Data defined*

Open Data can be any sort of data generated by companies, individuals, governments, and research organizations. The primary focus of most of the discussion over the past few years has been framed in the context of Open Data from federal or national governments, but data from governments is a small, but important, subset of the entirety of Open Data.

Gartner, the global technology consulting firm, defines Open Data in the following manner, "Open data is information or content made freely available to use and redistribute, subject only to the requirement to attribute it to the source. The term also may be used more casually to describe any data that is shared outside the organization and beyond its original intended use, for example, with business partners, customers or industry associations."[11]

The definition put forth by The Open Knowledge Foundation (OKF) begins with, "The Open Definition makes precise the meaning of 'open' with respect to knowledge, promoting a robust commons in which anyone may participate, and interoperability is maximized. Knowledge is open if anyone is free to access, use, modify, and share it—subject, at most, to measures that preserve provenance and openness."[12] For the complete, unabridged definition of Open data with all the related conditions for licensing and use, please refer to opendefinition.org.

Gartner's definition is limited to, and focuses on, commerce and sharing data as part of the processes of business. The OKF's definition provides a broad framework for all of society to develop Open Data upon and from. The only limitation or requirement in the OKF's definition is to be open or to share, and to attribute the data to the original source. In the OKF definition, there are no limitations on the application, integration, or use of the data.

Most of the Open Data community and advocates lean toward the OKF definition. Most of the organizations who outwardly and publicly support Open Data but do not actively work toward Open Data as a practical offering, tend to use the Gartner definition.

---

[11]"Open Data," *Gartner Glossary*, cited on Feb. 5, 2022, https://www.gartner.com/en/information-technology/glossary/open-data.

[12]"Open Definition 2.1," *Open Knowledge Foundation*, cited Feb. 5, 2022, https://opendefinition.org/od/2.1/en/.

6.5.2   *Open Data's beginnings*

Open Data as a term appeared for the first time in 1995, in a report from an American scientific agency. As explained by Simon Chignard, it dealt with the disclosure of geophysical and environmental data. "To quote the authors of the report: 'Our atmosphere, oceans and biosphere form an integrated whole that transcends borders.' They promote a complete and open exchange of scientific information between different countries, a prerequisite for the analysis and understanding of these global phenomena."[13]

Open Data evolved in conjunction and in parallel with the concept of open-source software (OSS). "OSS is computer software that is released under a license in which the copyright holder grants users the rights to use, study, change, and distribute the software and its source code to anyone and for any purpose. Open-source software may be developed in a collaborative public manner. Open-source software is a prominent example of open collaboration, meaning any capable user is able to participate online in development, making the number of possible contributors indefinite. The ability to examine the code facilitates public trust in the software."[14]

"In December 2007, thirty thinkers and activists of the Internet held a meeting in Sebastopol, north of San Francisco. Their aim was to define the concept of open public data and have it adopted by the US presidential candidates."[15] Among them was Lawrence Lessig, Professor of Law at Stanford University (California), who was "the founder of Creative Commons licenses, based on the idea of copyleft and free dissemination of knowledge."[16] Open Data came into being in the late 1990s and mostly evolved into its present form in the early 2000s.

6.5.3   *Open Data today*

In our discussion, we have focused on data that we generate from our activities—shopping on Amazon.com, browsing the web, clicking on advertising—but let's be explicit, it is not just numerical data that we are generating, it is all the posts we write, the blogs we author, the complaints we submit, the "likes" we click, the up/down votes we offer . . . *all* of the data we create.

Take a moment and apply that thought to all governments, companies, non-profits, and research organizations. A substantial portion of the data generated by those organizations, and the majority of data generated by individuals, could be designated as Open Data by the owners of the data, but *only* by the data owners.

The more organizations and people that designate their data as open, the more insights and intelligence that can be generated. Of course, we only want to designate data that can be used responsibly as open. Personal identifiable information (PII) will

---

[13]Simon Chignard, "A brief history of Open Data," *Paris Tech Review*, Mar. 29, 2013, cited on Feb. 6, 2022, https://www.paristechreview.com/2013/03/29/brief-history-open-data/.

[14]"Open-source software," *Wikipedia*, cited Feb. 6, 2022, https://en.wikipedia.org/wiki/Open-source_software.

[15]Simon Chignard, "A brief history of Open Data," *Paris Tech Review*, Mar. 29, 2013, cited on Feb. 6, 2022, https://www.paristechreview.com/2013/03/29/brief-history-open-data/.

[16]Ibid.

not be designated as Open Data, but data such as transactions, travel, and other data are perfect candidates to be marked as Open Data.

The OKF is a not-for-profit organization that works to bring about the use of Open Data on a global basis through teaching, building, and organizing. The mission of the OKF is "to create a more open world—a world where all non-personal information is open, free for everyone to use, build on and share; and creators and innovators are fairly recognized and rewarded."[17] It is worthwhile noting that the OKF's mission exempts personal information from their definition of *open*.

Often when analytics professionals are building analytical models, tools, and applications, there are questions from business professionals, lawyers, and others about how to protect personal information. For the most part, personal information is rarely, if ever, needed to build highly accurate and robust predictive models. In most cases, we, as analytical professionals, ask that personal identifiable information be removed from the data sets provided to us so that we never take possession of the personal data. That way we can never be questioned about the link between the predictive analytics results and personal data in the source data or information.

The Open Data movement, for the most part, has happened in the developed world in relation to federal and national data, and Open Data laws and regulations have been enacted in the majority of the US states as well.

The movement has benefited all of us, sometimes indirectly through greater transparency relating to governmental operations and programs, and sometimes directly. For example, most large US cities now have electronic signs that communicate when the next train, bus, or tram will arrive. This is due to the Open Data movement. There is more to be done at these levels and across the data sets that can potentially be offered as Open Data, but the processes are in flight, have momentum, and will not be stopped.

6.5.4 Governmental Open Data policies

Open Data, as it relates to national governments, means a subset of the data the government is responsible for that benefits people and society. Economics, jobs, road system efficiency, fiber-optic cable investments to improve internet access, building permits, school lunch programs, tree planting programs, etc, can unlock economic value and improve services. What is not included in Open Data from governments is personal data about individuals, identity information, data about national security, data related to the military, and data that would disadvantage individuals or groups.

A 2013 McKinsey report, *Open data: Unlocking innovation and performance with liquid information*, "identified more than $3 trillion in economic value globally that could be generated each year through enhanced use of open data—increasingly 'liquid' information that is machine readable, accessible to a broad audience at little or no cost,

---

[17]The Open Knowledge Foundation, cited on Feb. 5, 2022, https://okfn.org/.

and capable of being shared and distributed."[18] The sources of value from open data identified in the report include new or increased revenue, savings, and economic surplus in seven domains: consumer finance, consumer products, education, electricity, health care, oil and gas, and transportation.

The McKinsey research illustrates that governments are responsible for making the vast troves of data held in their systems available to the public, but they need to pass laws and regulations that foster and encourage Open Data across a number of sectors in their national economies. Three trillion dollars of economic output and activity is an astounding value. It takes a minute or two to wrap your mind around how much that actually is. The annual gross domestic product (GDP) of France in 2020 was 2.6 trillion dollars.[19] What McKinsey is saying is that we can add more than the output of France to the global economy each year by taking the necessary steps to make Open Data a reality on a widespread basis.

Data represents an incredible opportunity to create new value in existing industries—novel and innovative value. The data is here now, and it exists in a form that can be readily accessed and used today; we are just not using it as we could, and we as individuals are not being paid for the value that we create through our data.

Governments have many roles to play in making Open Data a reality across all sectors of our economies. Figure 6.1 shows the taxonomy McKinsey proposes for governmental roles and opportunities in relation to Open Data.

Provider
- Capture information electronically
- Release data publicly and regularly
- Identify ways to improve data quality

Catalyst
- Build an open-data culture
- Convene stakeholders
- Champion the movement

User
- Apply sophisticated analytics to improve decision making, offerings, and accountability
- Invest in people, tools, and systems

Policy maker
- Make rules for internal and external use
- Establish standards for data quality and format

Figure 6.1   Government can serve as an Open Data provider, catalyst, user, and policy maker to create value and mitigate risks.[20]

---

[18]Michael Chui, Diana Farrell, and Kate Jackson, "How government can promote open data," *McKinsey & Company*, Apr. 1, 2014, cited Jan. 30, 2022, https://www.mckinsey.com/industries/public-and-social-sector/our-insights/how-government-can-promote-open-data.

[19]"GDP (current US$)," *The World Bank*, cited on Feb. 5, 2022, https://data.worldbank.org/indicator/NY.GDP.MKTP.CD.

[20]Michael Chui, Diana Farrell, and Kate Jackson, "How Government Can Promote Open Data and Help Unleash Over $3 Trillion in Economic Value," *McKinsey & Company*, http://mng.bz/GR5q.

The Open Data Barometer (opendatabarometer.org) tracks the status of Open Data across 115 countries and jurisdictions and 15 categories of governmental data, including maps, land, statistics, budget, spending, companies, legislation, transport, trade, health, education, crime, environment, elections, and contracts.[21] According to the Open Data Barometer, the most active governments in fostering and creating an Open Data culture in their countries are Canada, Israel, Kenya, Korea, Mexico, and the UK (see figure 6.2). "The findings from the fourth edition of the Open Data Barometer show that while some governments are advancing towards these aims, Open Data remains the exception, not the rule. Why does this matter? Everyone should be able to access and use Open Data on an open web to allow them to participate fully in civic life. Without good data, it is impossible to hold governments to account for the decisions that they make, the policies they pass, and the money they budget and spend."[22]

Regional Rank	East Asia & Pacific		Europe & Central Asia		Latin America & Caribbean		Middle East & North Africa		North America		Sub-Saharan Africa	
	Global Rank	Score (/100)	Global Rank	Score (/100)	Global Rank	Score (/100)	Global Rank	Score (/100)	Global Rank	Score (/100)	Global Rank	Score (/100)
1	Korea 5th	81	UK 1st	100	Mexico 11th	73	Israel 28th	46	Canada 2nd	90	Kenya 35th	40
2	Australia 5th	81	France 3rd	85	Uruguay 17th	61	Tunisia 50th	32	USA 4th	82	South Africa 46th	34
3	New Zealand 7th	79	Netherlands 8th	75	Brazil 18th	59	UAE 60th	26			Mauritius 59th	26
4	Japan 8th	75	Norway 3rd	74	Colombia 24th	52	Kazakhstan 59th	26			Ghana 59th	26
5	Philippines 22nd	55	Spain 11th	73	Chile 26th	47	Qatar 74th	19			Tanzania 67th	22

Table 1: Barometer's fourth edition regional champions with their respective overall rankings and scores.

Figure 6.2   The most active governments in creating governmental Open Data[23]

---

[21]"GDP (current US$)," *The World Bank*, cited on Feb. 5, 2022, https://data.worldbank.org/indicator/NY.GDP.MKTP.CD.

[22]"Global Report, fourth edition," *Open Data Barometer*, cited on Feb. 5, 2022, https://opendatabarometer.org/4thedition/report/.

[23]Ibid.

Open Data is an economic imperative that can drive a level of value generation such that it can be a driving force in lifting sections of populations and younger generations out of poverty. Open Data needs to be ubiquitous across all governments and all relevant data, and it will be in the coming years.

Let's take a look at the Open Data initiatives in the US.

6.5.5   *Open Data: US federal and state governments*

The US federal government maintains a data.gov site for information about Open Data available from US government entities at the federal, state, and city levels.[24] The site includes links and access to Open Data resources for 48 US states, 48 US cities and counties, 53 international countries, and 165 international regions.

Map representation of Open Data Sites

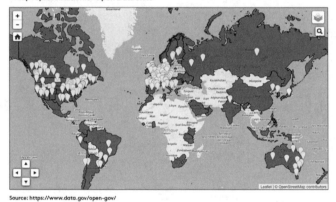

Source: https://www.data.gov/open-gov/

Figure 6.3   Global Open Data sites[25]

As you can see in figure 6.3, the majority of the governmental Open Data initiatives are in Western-style democracies. For the most part, dictatorships and autocracies are not supporters of Open Data initiatives.

In reviewing the Open Data site for the City of Chicago, I found a map that provides the locations of every establishment in Chicago that offers outdoor dining.[26] This is probably not useful from October to May, unless you possess a truly hardy constitution, but it's a great example of how Open Data can assist with everyday decisions like where to have lunch.

We are now starting to see new ways to share data in for-profit and not-for-profit offerings. A number of companies are working on data pools, data commons, and a significant number of healthcare and medically oriented data collections such as the UK Biobank and the US Cancer Consortium.

---

[24]"Open Government," *Data.gov*, cited on Feb. 6, 2022, https://www.data.gov/open-gov/.
[25]Ibid.
[26]"Dine al fresco with the Open Data Portal," Chicago Digital, cited on Feb. 6, 2022, https://digital.cityofchicago .org/index.php/dine-al-fresco/.

Figure 6.4   Al Fresco Dining locations in Chicago[27]

6.6   *Data exchanges*

Oliver Vagner described data exchanges this way in his September 2020 analysis and report, "The Rise of Data Exchanges": "Data exchanges are emerging as a key component of the data economy. By connecting data suppliers and consumers through a seamless experience, data exchanges have created a modern-day gold rush to help modern, digital organizations address their insatiable hunger for data. And, by eliminating the friction from finding, acquiring, and integrating data, these exchanges make it easy for any company to monetize its data assets and create new revenue streams."[28]

[27]Ibid.

[28]Oliver Vagner, "The Rise of Data Exchanges," Eckerson Group, September 2020, cited on Feb. 8, 2022, https://www.harbrdata.com/wp-content/uploads/2020/10/101220_Data_Exchanges_Harbr.pdf.

The first publicly available commercial data exchange available from a national government was announced on November 25, 2021, in Shanghai, China. A total of 20 data products were initially listed on the exchange, covering eight industries including finance, transportation, communication, and energy. "Xi Zenghui, deputy director of the internet department of State Grid Shanghai, said that the establishment of the Shanghai Data Exchange has made it possible to transform the company's electricity data into a value-added service. Based on the set of rules set at the exchange, State Grid Shanghai can provide processed data products that meet both data security requirements and buyer demand."[29]

The Shanghai Data Exchange was established to address the major difficulties in data trading, including identification of data ownership, pricing of data, reaching mutual trust between transaction parties, initiating transactions, and overall supervision, said local authorities.[30]

Commercial data exchanges are growing and evolving, and companies are already offering data exchange platforms so that companies can create their own data exchanges.

6.6.1   *Types of data exchanges*

All data exchanges collect, store, and manage data, but data exchanges differentiate themselves on the types of relationships that exist between the data exchange platform and the consumers of the data offered. There are three main types of data exchanges:

- *Peer-to-peer data exchange*—A peer-to-peer exchange facilitates direct data sharing between two companies that want to share data on a regular but episodic basis.
- *Private data exchange*—A private data exchange takes many forms. It could be an industry consortium, such as comparative raters, which collect and standardize insurance pricing data and distribute it to participating members and regulators. Also, a large company such as Wal-Mart or Target might use a private data exchange to share inventory data with their suppliers and collect shipment data in return.
- *Data marketplace*—A data marketplace is a public data exchange open to any company that wants to supply or consume data. Some marketplaces are global in scope, spanning every industry, function, and type of data.[31]

Clearly, it is early days for commercial data exchanges. The majority of the data offered is from existing list brokers from mailing lists, and other data that can be found in traditional direct mail brokers and other firms. Most of the activity in the areas that will contribute to the success and widespread offering of data exchanges are focused on providing data catalogs to commercial companies and augmenting those

---

[29]Shi Jing, "Shanghai launches data exchange," *China Daily*, Nov. 26, 2021, http://mng.bz/zm6a.
[30]Ibid.
[31]Oliver Vagner, "The Rise of Data Exchanges," Eckerson Group, September 2020, cited on Feb. 8, 2022, https://www.harbrdata.com/wp-content/uploads/2020/10/101220_Data_Exchanges_Harbr.pdf.

offerings with a collection of Open Data offerings collected from governmental sites around the world. There is a great deal of information on prison populations in numerous countries, but almost nothing on drive times in Dallas or other US cities.

It is clear that the data business needs to experience further evolution before we see widespread consumer value from these data collections and exchanges. However, it is encouraging to see this evolution being facilitated by the laws, regulations, and commercial development that is occurring across the European Union.

6.7 Data intermediaries, data pools, and data unions

In chapter 4 we reviewed the relevant global legislation that will enable individuals to control, share, and monetize their data. We looked briefly at the European Union's recent laws and regulations including the Data Governance Act (DGA), which is due to come into force in 2023. Among the various rights and frameworks created by the DGA, the portion of the legislation that is most relevant for our current discussion is the creation of data intermediaries.

"What's a Data Intermediary? The [DGA] legislation gives a good example: 'Data intermediation services would include ... data pools established jointly by several legal or natural persons with the intention to license the use of such a pool to all interested parties in a manner that all participants contributing to the pool would receive a reward for their contribution to the pool.'"[32]

Data intermediaries (DIs) are the organizations that will enable individualized data access; control; and the ability to direct your data to the aggregate data store or collective group that you feel will maximize your privacy, trust, revenue, and support for the organizations, companies, groups, or not for profits that you are aligned with.

You could decide that your data should be aggregated with people who buy products at Costco and Amazon. You may feel that this aggregation of data provides you with the greatest amount of revenue each year because you believe that the greatest number of companies will want to access, use, and analyze this data in aggregate.

Or perhaps you want to aggregate your browsing data across all the sites that you visit from your computer, mobile device, or applications with people who want to help Doctors without Borders. You want your data included in this group so that the staff at Doctors without Borders will know how to reach possible donors to the cause.

Given the characteristics of data, you can send all your data, or portions of your data, to as many or as few aggregations and groups within the data intermediary as you would like. If the terms are not working for you in any data group, change them. If you do not want your data to be used any longer, block access. If you do not want your data to be part of the aggregate or group any longer, delete your data from that group.

"Data intermediaries would act as cooperative or credit union-like structures that enable people to club their data together and sell it on their behalf. The union operators could take a cut of the sales but under the regulation they would have a fiduciary duty to their members to return value to them and act in their best interests. So,

---

[32]Shiv Malik, "The End of Data Monopolies," *Medium*, Jan. 20, 2022, http://mng.bz/0yox.

what's to stop a data intermediary/union from siloing the raw data once they've persuaded you to port it to them from Google and Amazon? The legislation [DGA] (see specifically Article 11.1) goes to some lengths to specifically ban data intermediaries from providing the sale of analytics from the same company that sells the raw data."[33]

One company that is working toward creating data unions that can be managed in a unified and consistent manner is Pool (www.pooldata.io). The founders state on their site, "It's no secret that the way data and privacy are managed and monetized is broken and unfair. To combat this, Data Unions have been created to give people control over their data—a well governed framework for dealing with personal information. . . . we created Pool to provide a marketplace and backend infrastructure so that Data Unions can scale quickly and data products from multiple organizations be conveniently queried, analysed and licensed—benefitting data buyers, and rewarding Data Union Operators and their members even more."[34]

The EU's DGA legislation enables the creation of data intermediaries and will create data unions where individuals can aggregate, share, and monetize their data. Commercial companies like Pool are creating data unions to enable the professional management of data unions. The ecosystem to provide control over our data is coming together quite well.

6.8   Data commons

"Data commons" is a term that has been used extensively in the healthcare and medical research fields. There are numerous examples of initiatives that stretch back to the mid-2000s. These are a few widely known commons:

- National Institute of Health Data Commons (https://commonfund.nih.gov/commons/awardees)
- The BloodPAC Data Commons (BPDC)—the leading repository for liquid biopsy data (www.bloodpac.org/)
- The BRAINCommons—a next-generation digital ecosystem that is uniquely able to meet today's data analysis challenges facing brain researchers (www.braincommons.org/)

While not called a data commons, one of the most widely known and utilized repositories of health data is the UK Biobank project. The UK Biobank is described as "a large-scale biomedical database and research resource, containing in-depth genetic and health information from half a million UK participants. The database is regularly augmented with additional data and is globally accessible to approved researchers undertaking vital research into the most common and life-threatening diseases. It is a major contributor to the advancement of modern medicine and treatment and has enabled several scientific discoveries that improve human health."[35]

---

[33]Ibid.

[34]"Data Working for Everyone," *Pool Portal*, cited Jan. 30, 2022, https://pooldata.io/.

[35]UK Biobank, cited Feb. 8, 2022, https://www.ukbiobank.ac.uk/.

The majority of data commons, repositories, and collections of available health data are collected, maintained, and managed with a goal of furthering research and developments into improvements for the health of all humanity.

The following are the goals from the National Cancer Institute's Cancer Research Data Commons:

- *Enable the cancer research community to share diverse data types across programs and institutions*
- *Provide secure access to data*
- *Facilitate the generation of innovative tools*
- *Help NCI-funded Data Coordinating Centers sustain and share data publicly*
- *Build in an open and modular way to make components extendable and reusable*
- *Adhere to FAIR principles of data stewardship: Findable, Accessible, Interoperable, and Reusable[36]*

These goals are similar to all the health data commons initiatives that I reviewed when researching data commons. There are a few organizations that require participants to pay on a cost-recovery basis (e.g., UK Biobank), all limit access to the data and samples to qualified researchers with bona fide and approved projects, and all adhere to the FAIR principles.

Data commons have proliferated around the world and are providing value to healthcare, medical research and development, and the health of people in general. Data commons will continue to grow in size and in the types of data that are collected for all aspects of human health.

Open Data, data pools, data exchanges, and data commons all came into existence in the past two decades. The ideas and concepts related to managing and using data are rushing forth with great speed and variation. As we move forward, we will see more creativity related to handling, using, and monetizing data.

6.9   Final thoughts

In this chapter we started by looking at the underlying research that created a new perspective on common resources and their management. That research and this new perspective has been applied to data and software. In the process, two completely new approaches to data and software have been created—open-source software (OSS) and Open Data.

OSS is one of the primary driving forces in the development of many types of software; it has changed the business and delivery models for software. Open Data is just beginning to receive the attention that OSS received in the early 2000s. National and pan-national governments have formulated and enacted laws that will enable Open Data to become Our Data. Individuals will be able to access, manage, control, and monetize their data in the near future.

---

[36]National Cancer Institute, "Cancer Research Data Commons," cited Feb. 8, 2022, https://datacommons.cancer .gov/cancer-research-data-commons.

This movement will take time to evolve and proliferate through the populations of the world, but it will happen. Data ownership is being redefined, and power over data is being given to those who create the data or pay for the creation of the data through their tax remittances.

Open Data is an evolving movement that has been well established in the large democracies in the West. The movement is evolving to include laws and regulations at the state and local levels. Access to all of the data that we create, and the data that is created by governments, will happen in the next few years. The EU started this process six years ago with the passing of GDPR and continues to drive the process that will transfer data ownership rights and the power to access, manage, delete, and monetize data to individuals. The current slate of EU legislation, including The Data Act, The Data Governance Act, and the Digital Markets Act provide for the legal frameworks, the processes, and the organizational structures needed to make individualized data ownership a reality in the foreseeable future.

We live in a world of ubiquitous and exponentially expanding data governed by norms and ideas that were formed 100 years ago. It is time to update our view of an asset that is readily available, incredibly valuable, and more versatile than any physical or electronic asset we have ever possessed. It is time to redefine how society views data and how we allocate the value derived from data.

It has been extremely exciting to see the evolution of the view of data in my professional career. When I started nearly 40 years ago, I would talk about the value of data, and people looked at me like I had six eyes. Once I had taken multiple data sets, integrated them together, and illustrated where buyers were, the optimum selling price for a product, or the best place to ship products, the skeptics became believers. Now, many years later, people around the world are aware of the value of data and want to change how the world manages and monetizes data. This is great.

By 2023, the Data Act, the Data Governance Act, and the Digital Markets Act will be in force. Numerous companies are already building products and services to support the change in data ownership and data monetization. By 2025 we will see real movement in the world market relating to the pricing, accessing, and managing of data.

Just think of it: your monthly data dividend arrives in your bank account without delay, and you can direct all it to your account, some of it to charities you support, or maybe some or all of it to your children or relatives. If you want more money, direct your data into higher earning aggregations and offerings. If you don't like what companies that have your data are doing, block access to your data, or better yet, charge them an exorbitant amount of money every time they access or use your data. You will be in control of every aspect of your data. Very exciting, isn't it?

Recently, after a court ruling that invalidated the existing data sharing agreement, the EU has been talking about changing the rules for transferring data to non-compliant countries. The US is a non-compliant country, and this change would be more restrictive regarding the data that could be transferred out of the EU jurisdiction. In response to this possibility, Meta has commented that they may stop offering

Facebook and Instagram in Europe.[37] What does that say to you? First, Meta is bluffing, and second, the Meta team is scared stiff of changing laws and policies related to data. That is a good place to have Meta and companies like them.

The EU laws that have passed and are on their way to being enacted will be blueprints for the rest of the world, just like the GDPR has been. Our data will be ours to control, use, and monetize as we wish. I am looking forward to having my share of that $3 trillion dollars in my bank account. Aren't you?

Very interesting things are happening with data beyond the raw data that you and I create from our activities and transactions. In the next chapter, we will discuss what data and analytics professionals are doing with our data that will extend the value that is created from our data for their organizations, clients, and for us.

Summary

- Open Data evolved from research that proved that common resource pools are managed more efficiently and effectively by groups that are involved and interested in the greater good than are resources managed by governments or profit-motivated organizations.
- Open Data is well established and is growing rapidly in national and state levels of governments around the world.
- Healthcare data is being donated and organized into data commons, mainly in the US and UK, and is proving a significant asset in making progress in healthcare research, drug development, and new cures and therapies.
- The GDPR provided the data foundation, and the Data Act, Data Governance Act, and data intermediaries are building on that foundation to create the new era of Our Data.
- In this new era of Our Data, each individual will be able to access, delete, manage, and monetize each and every piece of data that they create, own, and can benefit from.

[37]Sam Shead, "Meta says it may shut down Facebook and Instagram in Europe over data-sharing dispute," Feb. 7, 2022, https://www.cnbc.com/2022/02/07/meta-threatens-to-shut-down-facebook-and-instagram-in-europe.html.

Derived data, synthetic data, and analytics

7

This chapter covers

- Data lineage—where does data comes from and what data is used to create new data
- The escalating hierarchy of data from raw data to data used in optimization
- The current state of data generation—beyond human-created data to machine-generated data
- An Analytics Maturity Model illustrating analytics from simple dashboards to optimization

It ain't what you don't know that gets you into trouble. It's what you know for sure that just ain't so.[1]

—Mark Twain

---

[1] Mark Twain, "Quotable Quote," *Goodreads*, cited on Feb. 9, 2022, https://www.goodreads.com/quotes/7588008-it-ain-t-what-you-don-t-know-that-gets-you-into.

People who watch and analyze technology for a living—technology analysts, journalists, editors, practitioners, academics—discuss whether data or analytics is more important, as if the two are separable. They can be examined in isolation, but in the real world, if you want to make something of data or analytics, one requires the other for any meaningful activity to take place.

When you think of data, or when someone asks you about data, what do you think about? Do you see ones and zeros, text, or data in all its multiplicity of forms? Movies are data. This book is data. The conversation you recorded is data. Television programs are data. Self-driving cars and their navigational maps are data. Almost everything that you can talk about, think about, see, feel, and discuss has a data element associated with it. Almost everything that we do naturally creates data. We have a nearly limitless supply of data at our fingertips. With all this data, it would seem that we have more than enough data for all purposes. That is not the case.

In certain cases, typically limited to advanced analytics or modeling related to artificial intelligence, the use and analysis of data creates new and derivative data that has nothing to do with the original activity. In most cases there remains a relationship between the derivative data and the original activity, but the new data was not created from the original activity. The new data was and is a wholly new product typically created by an analytics process. Data moves, grows, and propagates beyond what we create. It is crucial that we manage, control, and protect our data so that we can be the primary beneficiaries of our data.

7.1   *Data lineage*

We first discussed data from gene sequencing in chapter 1 and we lightly touched on the concept of lineage at that point. *Data lineage* is the same as your genealogical lineage. When new data is created from existing data, or generated from raw, aggregated, or other natural sources of data, the new data has a lineage—a connection to the source or original data. Data lineage tracks back from the current data to all the data elements that were used to create the current data.

In most analytical applications, the data being used is an aggregation or a blend of many sources of data. To know how permissions, monetization, and compliance can be understood and be adhered to, we need to know what data has been used to create the new data assets.

Here's a quick example to illustrate the point: Unilever licenses my purchase data from me to analyze my buying behavior related to personal care products. Unilever then licenses my purchase data and blends it with data related to the purchasing and use of household cleaning products. Now we have two use cases where my data is licensed from me. Unilever needs to pay me to use my data in both analytical applications and process streams. To be able to track the payments correctly and to audit Unilever's use of my data, the data lineage needs to be created, tracked, analyzed, and monitored. In both use cases, the data Unilever licensed from me was blended with data from millions of other people, so data lineage is crucial to understanding how to track and monitor the data usage.

Several enterprise class data lineage products and platforms have been created and used in a wide range of industries. Tracking data lineage is not hard to do. It simply requires keeping records of how the data was created and where that data has been used. The new data world will create a new market for existing and expanded data lineage products and services.

7.2   Forms of data

Data has a life cycle. Most of us think of data being created as a direct or indirect result of our actions, such as browsing websites, buying items, watching videos, using apps, and playing games. That is only the beginning of data's life cycle.

Beyond its creation, data is aggregated, integrated, used as raw material to create new data, analyzed for patterns and then extended into newly created data, and much more. Once we create data, we have started an entirely new life cycle for this data and its derivatives.

7.2.1   Natural or raw data

Data occurs as a natural result of most of the processes we are involved in and, in the case of data created by automated machine processes, not involved in. The data that naturally occurs from browsing on a mobile device, a transaction at a store, or a weather element being recorded by a sensor is considered *natural* or *raw* data. It is data that is in its most granular and original form. It has not been added to any other data, or smoothed by an algorithm, or projected into the future. It is just a number that has been recorded to create a persistent indicator of an action or activity.

Natural or raw data is the beginning of all data. There are several common transformations that data undergoes as analytics professionals begin to attempt to understand, predict, prescribe, simulate, and optimize for desired outcomes. These transformations create new data that is beyond but related to natural or raw data.

7.2.2   Aggregated data

Data that is summed up into higher levels of abstraction is commonly referred to as *aggregated* data or *summarized* data. This is easy to understand, and most people do this intuitively. When I started in analytics, I worked at several CPG companies—Miles Labs, Coca-Cola, Pillsbury, Kraft, Anheuser-Busch, Cadbury-Schweppes. Each of them had their own aggregation hierarchies.

A simple example of a geographic aggregation hierarchy would be

Census block -> Zip +4 -> Zip code -> County -> State -> United States

Each of the lower levels are added or rolled up to obtain the information for the next level up in the hierarchy. There are many ways to aggregate data. Many people think about aggregating data through dimensions of data. Dimensions can include geography, product, price, promotions, distribution, gender, customers, patients, serving size, altitude, package size, color, and many more.

Often aggregated data is used in simple, but widely used, data reporting applications. Applications such as revenue reporting, budget planning, and promotions performance. The lineage of aggregated data is easy to understand, since it is endemic to the data and how the aggregation is created.

7.2.3 Derived data

Derived data is an extension of raw or naturally occurring data. In the process of creating derived data, analytics professionals take the naturally occurring data and extend it. Forecasted data is an example of derived data. Derived data is often the product of naturally occurring data being processed by an algorithm, or many algorithms, to extend the patterns found in the data into the future.

Store visits exhibit well-defined patterns. Even in anomalous conditions, store visits exhibit predictable behavior or patterns. In the US Midwest, when a storm is predicted, people go to the grocery store and buy staples like milk and bread at greater rates. Everyone in the area knows this, and that is why most people go to the store as soon as a storm is forecast. People new to the area always comment on the phenomena of stores being sold out of milk and bread just before a storm hits. It is like clockwork, predictable and expected.

Normal store visits have weekly, monthly, annual, seasonal, and holiday period patterns. With years of data available, these patterns are easy to discern. In forecasting, we combine the visit data—economic, crime, store expansion, store hours, population rates—and we can create derived data that illustrates the probable future visiting activity at the stores we are interested in. Not only can we forecast and derive data on the sales of an individual store, but we can derive and model data for all related stores, any planned new stores, and stores that may close. And not only can we forecast sales, but we can forecast and predict related metrics such as labor or staff scheduling, stocking rates, out-of-stock situations, and promotion effectiveness. All of these data streams are derived data—new data that we created.

In the new data world, derived data has a lineage connected to the visits and purchases we make at the stores, so we have an interest and ownership stake in the derived data and should be paid when the derived data is created and used. I expect that royalty payments for our part in derived data will be less than for naturally occurring data, but we will be paid, nonetheless. The generation of derived data not only gives us a view of the future, but it is also a stepping stone for the development of further types of new data.

7.2.4 Synthetic data

Synthetic data is created from our view of the world. We do not use existing data in the creation of synthetic data; we simply generate the data that we believe we need. Analytics professionals may want to understand how markets work or how markets might work, but given that no organization measures the activity we are interested in, we can create our own data that measures the market or activity.

Suppose a German retailer wants to build big box stores in Canada, the US, and Mexico in cities and towns where no big box store has ever existed. We would take on the project and begin by collecting all the relevant data that we could about the target cities and towns across the three countries. We would also collect data about big box stores from other retailers in existing cities in those three countries. We would also collect data related to the big box stores the German firm operates in other countries. We would collect, integrate, and analyze the various sources of raw and derived data to understand markets, stores, customers, and competition.

Then we would create our synthetic data about our proposed stores. In our example, the synthetic data is basically the inferences we have drawn from our analysis of the raw and derived data: optimal store size, product mix and pricing strategy to generate new sales, returns, pricing activity, and compensation costs. We would create synthetic data from scratch that will illustrate to our client which markets to select, how to phase the building of the stores, which locations are the best for each store, the store sizes, pricing strategy, and hiring strategy.

Much of the synthetic data created today is created by algorithms. Originally, we would create the data by hand, copying and extending data that we knew was close to or approximated the raw data. We would then move on to using rules-based systems to create data. Now we can use artificial intelligence to quickly and easily generate massive amounts of synthetic data that contains most if not all of the seasonality and other patterns that we see in naturally occurring data.

Of course, the ownership of the data is either with the consulting company or the client, depending on how the contract for the project was written. Synthetic data enables us to take the next step and begin to create a new type of data that blends naturally occurring data with our synthetic data, *simulations*, which create a new type of data—simulated data.

7.2.5 *Simulated data*

Simulations and *simulated* data enable us to create, analyze, and review an unlimited number of possible future scenarios. With the data collection, data generation, computing, and analysis capabilities that we have at our disposal, we can generate trillions of simulations.

Simulations enable us to put the scientific method on steroids. We can change each variable or combination of variables in any way we wish. Make a small change in one variable and rerun the simulation. Make a large change in another variable, and rerun the simulation. Make a specific family of changes in a specified group of variables, and rerun the simulation. Most people will know this approach as a Monte Carlo simulation. As I noted earlier, we can run an unlimited number of changes, analyze all the results, and find the optimal scenario.

This may sound like a manual process. It can be, and it was in the past, but now, using a large capable computer, we can develop complex, multi-step processes that simulate real world activities. We can build simulation scenarios that play out millions, billions, and trillions of sequences and interactions in a few hours.

Before running the simulations, we ask the client about their primary objectives—whether they include understanding and planning for the following:

- Maximum number of stores in a defined time frame?
- Optimal number of stores in selected markets?
- Best mix of stores that will be returning maximum profit in the shortest time possible?
- Maximum number of stores in the top-performing markets?

Once we know their primary and secondary and maybe even tertiary objectives, we can set up the testing variables and scenarios and run the simulations. Out of the trillions of scenarios, we can easily see where our client needs to focus. We then collaborate with our client to suggest where to start buying property, how much money to invest, and how quickly to build stores.

Most organizations run the required or desired simulations, find the optimal outcome, and discard the simulations. However, the outcomes of all the scenarios in the simulations are valuable data that has taken time, effort, and cost to construct; why would you discard this data?

When I am executing consulting work, I ask for the rights to the simulation data, and most people are happy to sign those rights over to my consulting firm. If I am employed at a full-time job and I oversee this type of work, I ensure that all the data is archived for future reference or use.

Simulation data has a small amount of lineage, tracing back to some of the source data we collected as input into the simulation runs. It could be argued that the creators of the source data are due compensation for the use of their data, but the amount of compensation would be very small. Each time we use data that is multiple steps removed from the outcome, the data ownership, and the importance of the input data to the outcome is lessened, so the monetary compensation for the use of the data is also reduced.

7.2.6 *Optimization data*

In optimization software, processes, projects, and programs, analytics professionals are looking to find not only the optimal combination of inputs and contextual variables, and the best use of competing resources, we are also attempting to find, verify, and present the best possible path forward for our business colleagues or consulting clients.

Optimization data is the data that is generated in the quest to find those best-fitting business, market, and operational conditions. Every source and type of data we have discussed can be input into optimization systems and processes. The most important data input in the optimization process is the data from the simulation processes that we just discussed. Analytics professionals further refine, enrich, and extend data to continue moving up the ladder of analytics to deliver deeper insights and more accurate predictions and recommendations to our business compatriots.

Optimization processes are like simulation processes in that we can optimize for objectives that interest our client or colleagues. We can set up automated processes to vary the conditions and run the optimization software an unlimited number of times to consider all the conditions, even the most unlikely, that are expected to have an impact on the projects considered.

Simulations and simulated scenarios illustrate what is possible. Optimizations prescribe or tell the business executives and managers which of those scenarios is most likely to deliver on their stated objectives and goals. Just as predictive and prescriptive analytics work in tandem, so do simulations and optimizations. The first illuminates all the possibilities, and the latter informs the relevant professionals as to the best path forward. The data that results from the optimization process is also like that from the simulation processes—it should be saved and used in future projects. Data has costs. The more work and effort that goes into creating data, the more valuable that data is. All data should be saved and be used in future analytics projects and programs if possible.

7.2.7   *Machine-generated data, Internet of Things data*

Historically, when data was generated, there was a person involved purchasing, browsing, talking, texting, typing, etc. All data was created in conjunction with a human or humans driving the effort. Over the past decade, however, more data has been created without any human involvement. "70% of the world's data is probably going to be created and acted upon outside of data centers in the future, meaning in edges. . . . And so the one kind of last threshold to cross, I think, to really accelerate the entire ecosystem forward is people have to start to get comfortable and lean into this idea that inevitably the future is a much different balance between the work that people and the work that machines will do."[2]

In short, most data that is created will soon be created without any human intervention. The data will be created in machine-to-machine interfaces, and it will be created, stored, managed, used, and analyzed without any humans being in the loop.

The *Internet of Things (IOT)* is a collection of sensors, devices, and other machines that generate data without any intervention by machines or humans. Much of the data is highly repetitive, mechanistic, and rather useless, but when things start to go wrong, the automated monitoring of the data stream can be useful in preventing failure, costly maintenance, theft, or catastrophic loss.

With light bulbs, vending machines, roads, cars, single machines in factories all producing data at the millisecond level, it is no surprise that there will be an overwhelming abundance of this type of data. We as individuals and as organizations do not need this level of detail, but automated monitoring, proactive alerting, and the capturing of unusual patterns can help make operations in factories, stores, roads, bridges, and many other areas of our daily lives safer, easier, and less costly.

As the amount of data increases exponentially, much of it is already machine generated, machine read, summarized, and stored. Much of this data will not be acted upon or reviewed by people.

---

[2] Laurel Ruma, "To accelerate business, build better human-machine partnerships," *MIT Technology Review*, Dec. 13, 2021, cited March 5, 2022, https://www.technologyreview.com/2021/12/13/1041888/to-accelerate-business-build-better-human-machine-partnerships/.

Remember the point made earlier: the more work that goes into creating and managing data, the more value that is embedded in that data. The value quotient of highly curated data is much higher, whereas the value quotient of machine-generated data is quite low.

7.3 Analytics and data

When people ask me about my career and work, I usually say that I am involved in data and analytics. The follow-up questions usually are related to analytics. Very few people ask about data, but without data there are no analytics. Given that advanced analytics and artificial intelligence are top of mind for many people, it might be helpful to review common analytics approaches.

The most misused term in business at this time is analytics. People say "analytics" when they are talking about dashboards and simple reporting. They say "analytics" when they are talking about descriptive statistics. These are misleading uses of the word "analytics." Analytics starts when the analytical approaches have advanced mathematics, algorithms, and some type of learning involved.

7.3.1 Analytics continuum

Earlier I remarked that I did not view the early stages of the analytics continuum as true analytics, and I still hold this to be true, but I want to include these early stages so it's clear where the analytics continuum begins. I want to illustrate the genesis of data and the rudimentary steps of data creation, data cleaning, and simple reporting—all steps that are necessary and precede analytics.

Figure 7.1 outlines the overall analytics continuum.

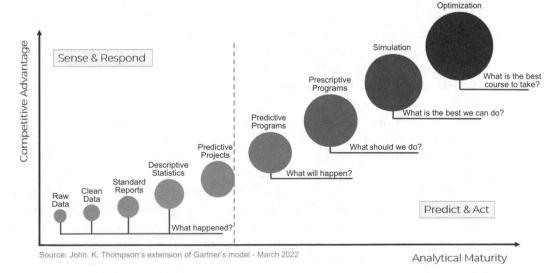

Figure 7.1   Analytical Maturity Model—John K. Thompson, March 2022

7.3.2   *Stage 0: Descriptive statistics*

Descriptive statistics are the statistical methods that we learned in high school and college. These are statistical techniques like averages—means, modes, and Gaussian distributions. Data scientists use these tools to create an exploratory data analysis (EDA). Data scientists use the results of the EDA phase of a project to illustrate to executives, senior managers, subject matter experts (SMEs) and others the state of the business operations as seen through data.

Often business managers rely on their historical understanding of the business rather than on a true understanding of the current, actual operations. In a recent project we illustrated to the business managers that the way they viewed a subset of the operations as having special characteristics related to a segment of the customer population was out of date and inaccurate. Over the past 10 years, the organization had stopped marketing to this segment of the customer population. As a result, the population in the segment stopped visiting the organization's branches. It took more than six months to convince the relevant management that they could reengage this population, but that they had to develop and deploy new marketing and pricing programs to do so.

I do not consider this step to be analytics. This is simple reporting and statistics. It is preparation work required to move everyone to the same level of understanding and to pave the way for the real work of analytics.

7.3.3   *Stage 1: Predictive analytics*

Predictive analytics uses historical data to illustrate patterns of actions, behaviors, and transactions to understand how businesses operate, how people interact, how supply chains work, and how price affects behavior.

Data scientists bring together multiple sources of related data to create one or more models that produce results that are as close as possible to how the world actually works. That is the primary objective of predictive analytics: to build a model or a stream of models that take data and predict as accurately as possible what the future of that business process or business environment will look like.

Data scientists bring these data sets together and create features that feed into models. Features can be raw or natural data, aggregated data, derived data, synthetic data, or any combination of the varying types of data we have discussed. The goal of predictive analytics is to predict what will happen in the future with the best possible accuracy.

Historical data is crucial to being able to predict the future. We need to understand the past and describe the environment we are interested in with sufficient detail so that we can understand how the features drive change in the actions and behaviors in the environment. With reliable, sufficient, varied, and accurate historical data, data scientists can predict with solid accuracy what will happen and when it will happen.

Over the past 50 years, we have gotten much better at predicting the future. We can generally predict with acceptable accuracy what will happen and when it will happen in the next 24 months. Further out than 2 years, error rates begin to creep up, and we need to be careful of our level of reliance on numerical predictions.

7.3.4   Stage 2: Prescriptive analytics

Prescriptive analytics is an extension of predictive analytics. As data scientists gather and create a significant amount of data, they save predictions from the predictive analytics and aggregate them to enable analyses of the success, efficacy, and value of those predictions. They then create prescriptive models that recommend the best predictions to follow or to act upon, out of the various predictions that have been made.

Prescriptive models prescribe the actions that business executives, managers, and subject matter experts should take. Over the past 15 years we have gotten better at understanding how to take predictive data and create prescriptive applications and outcomes from that data. Prescriptive applications and models are not widely used in business today. Not many business executives understand and support the resources needed to design, build, and maintain prescriptive environments.

Market leading firms in numerous industries do employ prescriptive models and applications. The investments by these firms, coupled with their supportive view of data, analytics, and innovation, is part of the reason that they are in market-leading positions.

7.3.5   Stage 3: Simulation

Based on the data used in the prediction and prescription efforts, data science teams build simulation systems that enable business users to vary their assumptions and plans. The simulation system is run many times to see which of their plans, ideas, and visions produce the best business outcomes.

Some simulation environments enable and empower business professionals to input a few variables to see how operations will respond. It is easy for business users to vary the inputs, like price, promotions, program time boundaries, products, and the number of customers involved, to receive real-time responses that illustrate whether this combination of variables will generate the desired response. Other simulation environments enable end users to set up complex scenarios that unfold over time. This provides a picture of business and process performance as the predetermined variables are injected into the simulated environment.

These simulation environments enable business managers to gain confidence that they are seeing the projected performance of markets, companies, products, and customers in a safe environment. Business managers can try sets of plans and variables that they have seen before in real-world markets. They can validate that the models are producing accurate results and empower business users to create new and interesting scenarios delivering a competitive advantage.

Simulation systems have been evolving over the past 50 years. We have seen a few approaches, like system dynamics,[3] that have been developed, discredited, and

---

[3] "System Dynamics Society," *Wikipedia*, cited Mar. 7, 2022, https://en.wikipedia.org/wiki/System_Dynamics_Society.

discarded, and others that are multi-model and multi-modal and that have proven to be very effective at simulating real-world activity with low error rates. Digital twins are an area of simulation that is being widely used and that has provided significant benefits to organizations around the world.[4]

7.3.6   *Stage 4: Optimization*

The final and most advanced stage of analytic sophistication that we see in commercial environments today is optimization models and applications. Optimization models and applications build on all the preceding levels of data and analytics sophistication that we have discussed.

Predictive and prescriptive models and applications work in a positive reinforcing cycle of automated improvement, and simulation and optimization applications work in a similar cycle of automated positive reinforcing improvement. If an organization saves and manages the outputs of their simulation models and applications, that highly refined, rich data can be the input into optimization models and applications. The optimization environment then becomes an AI-based system that enables executives, business managers, and subject matter experts to see well into the future—much further than their competitors ever could.

Optimization models and applications analyze the billions and trillions of simulations and recommend the course of action that is best aligned with the business outcomes and objectives, as stated by the business executives, managers, and subject matter experts.

Academic institutions and leading commercial firms have been experimenting with optimization systems. These systems are not widely used; they are difficult to build and are complex to operate. These systems are the focus of some of the most advanced technical minds in business and academia. Optimization systems hold much promise in the future, but there is much development to be completed before we will see widespread deployment and use of these advanced systems in everyday corporate use. If your firm is building or using an optimization environment, you are in the small, leading minority of firms.

7.4   *Augmented intelligence*

Augmented intelligence is a symbiosis of human and artificial intelligence working together to enable an organization to make better, more informed decisions through data and sophisticated models and modeling.[5] Humans are very good at pattern recognition, intuition, and recalling the entirety of a situation that they have experienced before. Computers are very good at processing massive amounts of data to find the optimum outcome and which input variables and features are combined in a very specific way to achieve those outcomes. In business and society, we need to move to an evolved

---

[4] "Digital twin," *Wikipedia*, cited Mar. 7 2022, https://en.wikipedia.org/wiki/Digital_twin.
[5] Judith Hurwitz, Henry Morris, Candace Sidner, and Daniel Kirsch, *Augmented Intelligence: The Business Power of Human–Machine Collaboration* (Auerbach Publications, 2019).

position that has a deeper level of comfort with and a better understanding of how humans and computers can work together to complement each other.

7.5   Data scientists and statisticians

There is no doubt, we need more analytically oriented people. But we also need the right analytically oriented people in the right roles if we are to reach our goals in understanding business operations and driving improvement in those operations through data and analytics.

I manage teams of data scientists, developers, data engineers, data visualization experts and user interface and user experience (UI/UX) designers. One of our primary goals is to build analytical applications that will enable business users to engage with the data, models, algorithms, and interfaces to analyze, understand, and improve business performance easily, quickly, and immediately.

In the process of filling openings for data scientists, I have seen several colleagues ask me if they should hire a statistician to fill a data science opening. Statisticians are great. They are numerate, well-trained, good at following rules, and they love to work with data. Sounds like a good fit, no? No, it is not.

Statisticians are trained to use statistics. That is good for functions in chemistry labs, research and development, and many other functions where you simply want to know if the data fits the purpose and is within the stated parameters. Statisticians, for the most part, are looking for certainty. They want to include or exclude conditions, situations, and factors as soon as possible. They are very good at their jobs, and it serves both them and the organization for them to be roles where compliance, certainty, and process are keys to success.

Data scientists are creative; they are looking for ways that the data can help improve the business, change a market, bring in more customers, or execute a business change that will take performance to an entirely new level. Data scientists are innovators, creators of change, drivers of transformation. We do not want statisticians to be data scientists, and the reverse is true as well. There are roles for both, and we need and want both, but let's not confuse the two.

Do not hire a data scientist to execute purely statistical work, and do not hire a statistician to be a data scientist. If you do, you will be unhappy, because the work you need completed won't be, and you will have a short-term employee when they realize they were hired to do work that they have little or no interest in.

Not all analytics personnel are the same. If you want to delve more deeply into understanding analytics professionals, please read my book, *Building Analytics Teams: Harnessing analytics and artificial intelligence for business improvement.*[6]

---

[6] John K. Thompson, *Building Analytics Teams: Harnessing analytics and artificial intelligence for business improvement* (Packt Publishing, 2020).

7.6 *Final thoughts*

This chapter has enabled us to slightly open our view to examine topics that are data-related. In this chapter, I wanted to take a bit of time to outline topics that are important to the future of data and to provide a bit of a framework to hold the context for our view of the new world of data.

The world of data is fascinating and enables us to peer into the future. We can take data in its native form and do so many insightful things with it. We can tell why people act in a certain manner, we can understand the reality of numerous situations when, in many cases, the exhibited behavior seems counter to what we would expect. Data in its raw form is interesting and provides for exciting insights, but it is also limited in what it can tell us. The new forms of data that we reviewed in this chapter are the foundations on which we can peer into and, in many cases, predict the future.

When I started working with data, I immediately began to sum it up, twist it around, and look at it in new ways: invert it, integrate it, and project it into the future. One of the wonderful things about data is its flexibility and extensibility. Yes, a great deal can be and is accomplished with naturally occurring or raw data, but even more is accomplished with extended data sets.

Summarized data, integrated data, projected data, derived data, synthetic data: all are tools that we, as analytics professionals, use every day. Not many people know or think about these data types. They may be esoteric, but they are not hard to understand. They are simply specialized tools that help us understand the world today and the world that will be here very soon, whether in minutes, weeks, days, months, or possibly years.

So far, over the course of this book, we have

- Reviewed the history of data: the people, reasons, and factors that have been responsible for creating the data ecosystem that we have inherited
- Examined the human elements of trust and privacy that form the natural law and, by extension, the body of law that will provide the foundation for the new data ecosystem that is evolving and will be here very soon
- Gotten a glimpse into what data and analytics professionals do with our data to predict, prescribe, simulate, and optimize what will happen in the near future.

We now know a little of what happens with our data, from creation to its many use cases. We also know what spawns from our data, and where it might go and what it can create.

Summary

- The data ecosystem begins with raw or naturally occurring data that is generated from all human activities.
- Data extends from raw data and is transformed and extended into aggregated or summarized data, integrated data, derived data, synthetic data, simulated data, and optimization data.

- All data has a lineage that enables the tracking and tracing of the creation and integration of data.
- Data and analytics are intertwined. The Analytics Maturity Model (figure 7.1) illustrates the increasing stages of analytical sophistication from predictive analytics to optimization.

Looking forward:
What's next for our data?

This chapter covers

- The incredible potential for positive change related to our data that mostly benefits us

- The possibility for data solutions to be very simple or quite profound, depending on our viewpoint

- New business sectors, products, and services related to the new world of individualized control and monetization of data

- The relationship and activities you will manage through a data intermediary (DI)

- What is a data dividend, and how much money will you make from your data

- What you can do with your data settings today to be ready for the new future data ecosystem

---

Agathism: The doctrine that, in the end, all things tend toward good. . . . An optimist would say that everything is for the best. An agathist, on the other hand, would say that what's happening right now may be unfortunate or evil, but, ultimately, it will all end well.[1]

—Anu Garg

---

[1] Anu Garg, "Agathism," *A.Word.A.Day*, Dec. 27, 2021, https://wordsmith.org/words/agathism.html.

8.1 Where do we go from here?

In the previous chapters we discussed what the world of data looks like, how we got to where we are, and what the world looks like today. Now it is time to discuss what lies *ahead.*

As with most changes in the world, data won't change in a big bang. Not all factors will change in an instant. The world at large—laws, regulations, enforcement, business operations, attitudes, and compliance—will not change in the blink of an eye. All of the changes that I am about to describe will come in waves and will be enforced and reinforced over time.

8.1.1 National and state laws will lead and guide the changes

Businesses will comply and individuals will align with policies and new norms that benefit them. However, businesses and individuals will push back against changes they do not understand or view as being against their better interests.

This will be one of the most significant legal, social, and economic changes in our lifetimes, on par with the creation and commercialization of the internet. We are talking about the recognition of a new asset class that's already owned, but without the legal, social, business, and operational infrastructure to delineate and designate ownership or to manage and monetize appropriately.

Our data has been, up until now, appropriated by business without our permission. This is changing, and that change will impact everything that we do and know.

8.1.2 The new data ecosystem will create and realign flows of money

In chapter 6 I, referenced the McKinsey report, *Open data: Unlocking innovation and performance with liquid information*, which "identified more than $3 trillion in economic value globally that could be generated each year through enhanced use of open data—increasingly 'liquid' information that is machine readable, accessible to a broad audience at little or no cost, and capable of being shared and distributed."[2] The sources of value from open data identified in the report include new or increased revenue, savings, and economic surplus in seven domains: consumer finance, consumer products, education, electricity, health care, oil and gas, and transportation.

There will be intense competition to capture the initial wave of value and money. There will also be a surge to set up businesses and operations that will profit from, support, and sustain the affiliated industries, operations, businesses, connections to governments, business services, consumer services, and more.

8.1.3 Innovation and change will create friction and opportunity

Dr. Carlotta Perez explained the technological, sociological, and economic dynamics well in her 2002 book, *Technological Revolutions and Financial Capital.* Dr. Perez stated,

---

[2] Michael Chui, Diana Farrell, and Kate Jackson, "How government can promote open data," April 1, 2014, *McKinsey & Company*, https://www.mckinsey.com/industries/public-and-social-sector/our-insights/how-government-can-promote-open-data.

In order for the techno-economic paradigm to take effect, changes have to happen within the society. The new technology that comes with the technological revolution has to be accepted by society. The new products, the new services have to have consumers and users, without them the innovative technology would not take over and become a technological revolution that needs a new set of rules and common-sense bases to organize the activities. The changes in technology will eventually bring changes in governance, society, ideologies, and culture, they will include changes in regulatory frameworks affecting markets and economic activities, they will redesign a whole lot of institutions (government organizations, companies), there will be a need for new financial regulations and education. Society is opposed to the new set of rules and ways of doing things, even though they were received as a bright new set of opportunities because it is recognized as a threat to the established way of doing things in society, firms, and institutions. The changes are faster in the economy because there the profits and growth are driving the change, it is not the case within the society. The blockage is caused by routine, ideology, and vested interests and that takes time to change. The social tensions are even multiplied by great social costs in the form of lost jobs and skills as well as moving operations from one place to another.[3]

8.1.4   *It may be hard to see, but change is well underway*

Governments at the national, state, provincial/regional, and local levels are taking their lead from the EU. The GDPR was the blueprint for the data rights of all citizens, and it established the framework of responsibility and accountability for all companies. The Data Act and the Data Governance Act (discussed in chapters 2 and 4) will have the same or greater impact, and the ripple effect will produce further legislation on a global basis. New laws are in process, and this change is certain to happen on all governmental levels, first in the western-style democracies and then spreading around the world to all societies. In business, these are just a few of the firms and offerings that will be created or expanded to service and support the new data economy:

- Additions to legal firms and possibly the creation of specialist legal firms that are founded to help businesses and consumers interpret the new laws and regulations at the national, state, and local levels in numerous countries.

- New consulting firms or new practices in existing consulting firms to support enterprise-class companies on how to manage the aspects and elements of the newly emerging data ecosystem and to become and remain compliant with all relevant laws.

- Technology and data-specialist companies that will create new data monetization platforms that existing companies can subscribe to, so they do not have to build such a system themselves.

- An entire industry built to manage the data from a physical data perspective. Security of the data will be paramount. New systems with security at the heart of their operation and design will be created.

---

[3] Carlota Perez, *Technological Revolutions and Financial Capital: The Dynamics of Bubbles and Golden Ages* (London: Elgar, 2002).

- Companies that offer monetization programs that fit the financial, social, and philanthropic goals of individuals, groups, families, and more.
- Companies to manage the resulting and required aspects of financial payments for data access and use will need to be created.
- Companies that will either build an independent platform allowing people to access, manage, and delete their data, or that will build systems for companies that want their own platforms, or both.
- Companies have already been created to define and manage the relationship between individuals and their data (Pooldata.io and others).

Lawyers and accountants will see new business arise as consumers seek guidance. Individuals will want access to their data as well as monetization programs to set up their relationship with their data. They will want to manage the dynamic relationship between them and their raw data, data aggregations, monetization settings, data retention, and destruction settings.

Consumers will want guidance on how to achieve their objectives related to revenue maximization, optimal charitable giving, supporting specific companies, disincentivizing other companies, and sharing data without monetary compensation. Companies will provide these services online via mobile apps.

It may be hard to conceive of such a sea change in how data will be viewed, managed, and leveraged, but we have seen this before. When Steve Jobs and Bill Gates said that we would all have at least one computer in our houses, many scoffed. When the first handheld devices were announced, many wrote them off as mere toys and distractions. Electric cars had the same reaction. There are numerous venture capital firms, private equity funds, entrepreneurs, lawmakers, and other interested parties making investments in these areas. While it may seem far-fetched today, in a few short years it will seem as if it was always meant to be this way, because it was.

We are talking about an entire global industry being created. This is nothing short of groundbreaking and game changing. Our world is just catching up with reality.

8.2 A day in the life of your data . . . well, actually two days

In chapter 2 we walked through what happens to, and with, your data today. We examined how your everyday activities create data, where that data travels, where the data is stored, who has access to the data, what companies do with your data, how they sell your data, and the minuscule amount of value that you receive for your data. We are all aware of the current life cycle of our data.

8.2.1 Data you create each day will not change

The data created from all your activities, whether they are originated or executed on a laptop, desktop, mobile device, handheld, tablet, or any other electronic device, are virtually the same. Also, the data journey is virtually the same whether you are using an online service via a browser or a mobile app on a portable device. We will not be delineating the differences arising from using particular devices or services in this journey.

The device, or service, or app you use for the various activities in your normal daily activities are relevant from the perspective of your data, but virtually the same for this discussion.

In outlining what will happen with our data in the future, we are assuming the following:

- The current trend in consumer sentiment against being tracked, targeted, and messaged with irrelevant offers, messages, and divisive content will continue to be of concern to a significant portion of the population.
- The current momentum of developing, passing, and enacting laws enabling individual access, control, and monetization of data will continue to evolve in substantially the same direction it has over the past six years and will continue to proliferate and expand to all levels of government.
- For-profit companies, venture-capital firms, private-equity funds, other investors, and governments will continue to engage with and invest in the process of developing the required infrastructure to enable individual data access, data management, data monetization, payment processing, and related capabilities.
- The number of technology and computing options for storing, securing, managing, accessing, and monitoring data will continue to grow, evolve, and proliferate. This discussion is not focused on technology choices, computing architecture, or other technology details.

8.2.2   *All the data we create in our daily lives: An example*

I am taking a road trip and my wife, Jennifer, is with me. We are driving from Chicago to Ann Arbor to pick up our daughter from the University of Michigan. We decided that we would use a map and navigation service accessed via my mobile device rather than the navigation system in the car. I like the map and navigation voice feature from the online service. It sounds better than the voice in the car. I know that I can customize the voice feature of the car navigation system, but doing so is too cumbersome. Also, I like the intervals at which the map and navigation service calls out upcoming turns, detours, and speed traps. In my opinion, the additional services offered by the online map and navigation system are superior to the navigation system in the car. I bring up the map and navigation service on my mobile device and start to drive.

The navigation service is notifying us about suggested routes, road conditions, available roadside services, road construction (of which there is a lot during the spring and summer months), detours, emergency services, hospitals, police presence, and posted speed limits. We may even get weather alerts as we travel across Illinois, Indiana, and Michigan. These are all very useful pieces of information when making decisions about beginning the drive, and along the way as well. Through the map and navigation service, we are providing data about our route of travel, location, speed, use of roadside services, departure time, and arrival time.

Through the in-car systems, we provide data about the following:

- Braking actions
- Lane changes
- Reactions to any police presence
- Use of turn indicators
- Overtaking maneuvers
- Safe or unsafe following distances
- Acceleration rates
- Parking preferences
- Energy consumption
- Use of charging stations
- Degradation of system functionality
- Impending subsystem failures

From our in-cabin settings, we provide the following data:

- Environmental controls (seat warmers, temperature, fan speed)
- Touch screen interaction rates
- Music preferences
- Incidence of distracted driving
- Use of autopilot
- Incidence of car intervention during driving
- Driver profile changes along the route
- Automation of actions, like having the car close the garage door without pressing a button

Jennifer, the passenger on our journey, is providing data through her mobile device:

- Browsing activity
- Songs played
- Pictures taken along the way
- Phone calls to tell our daughter where we are in the trip
- A visit to the online ordering feature of a restaurant in Ann Arbor
- A reservation for dinner in Ann Arbor
- A few text messages coordinating activities
- Purchases on Amazon for things that popped up in conversation

From our activities in the physical world, we are providing yet more data:

- Tolls paid through a prepaid transponder or cash/credit/debit for toll payment
- Where we stopped for gas and snacks
- How much we bought and what we paid

- The payment method used, which could involve the redemption of loyalty points
- Whether I accepted in-pump offers
- What ads I saw on the pump screen
- Whether local activities like the weather make a difference in my experience at the pump
- Whether my purchase is in line with other purchases that I made in the US, the UK, and Western Europe
- Video footage of our movements through the store
- Whether we used the restroom

In some cases, we drive up, have lunch, load up the car with our daughter and her stuff, and then drive back to Chicago. For the sake of this discussion, let's assume that we are staying the night in Ann Arbor, and that Jenifer and I are attending the Michigan football game the next day.

We arrive in Ann Arbor, check into the hotel where we are members of the loyalty program. We are greeted by name, are given our arrival amenities, are asked about our room preference, which the staff already knows, are given the two rooms keys, which we always ask for, are told that we have an early check-in, that our room is ready, and that the room that we prefer was available and has been reserved for us. Our request for a late check-out has been confirmed, and we are asked if we want a ride to the stadium tomorrow, which we do request.

After taking a break from traveling, we text our daughter, pick her up, and go over to the restaurant, where we have a reservation that Jennifer made on the drive to Ann Arbor. We take a few pictures, which are shared in our family group chat. We order our drinks, appetizers, entrees, and dessert, all of which is entered into a mobile device (i.e., a handheld or tablet) by a member of the restaurant staff. The staff takes a couple of pictures for us, and those are shared in the group chat as well. The check arrives, we decide upon the tip amount based on the quality of the service, we pay via credit card, and we thank the restaurant staff members who helped us have a lovely dinner.

We take our daughter back to her apartment. She will continue the evening with friends, as college students do, and, of course, all her activities will be documented on her mobile device through text messages, pictures, and location data. Jennifer and I go back to the hotel, pick up our water for the evening, go to our room, and retire for the day.

Since arriving in Ann Arbor, we added to the data stream, including more location data, V2V interactions and data, V2I interactions and data, additional pictures, texts, voicemails, emails, hotel arrival and check in data. We confirmed our preferences for check-in and check-out times, added to our loyalty points in the hotel program and to our dining history and preferences, confirmed and added to our tip history. If the hotel has smart locks, we also confirmed that we called it a day, early.

We wake up and call room service to order breakfast. We put the charge on our room bill, along with the tip. We text our daughter to set up a place to meet. We meet at the M Den to buy an additional sweatshirt, since the weather is colder than was forecast. We walk over to the stadium, scan our tickets on our mobile devices, and go to our seats. The game is raucous, fun, and enjoyable. Our location data puts us not only in the stadium, but in a specific section. We exit the stadium, walk back to the hotel, load up our belongings, check out of the hotel, pick up our daughter, and drive home.

We generate an incredible amount of data. Nearly all our actions are captured by some sort of electronic infrastructure. Once I started to examine each activity and the data generated from those actions, I was amazed. After I realized that all this data was being created and captured, I had a range of emotions from being a bit freaked out to being really excited as a data and analytics professional, and over time I became convinced that I would need to write this book to help others understand the implications of creating all of this data each and every day.

8.2.3   *New data streams from our roads and cars*

By 2023 there will be small, experimental stretches of road in Michigan, Sweden, Israel, and Italy that charge electric cars as they drive. "The roadway will charge electric vehicles whether they're in motion or at a stop through a process called inductive charging, which uses a magnetic frequency to transfer power from metal coils that are buried under the road to a special receiver on the underside of the electric vehicles. ... the road will operate normally for all gas cars and electric vehicles that are not equipped with the receiver."[4]

The US government, through the National Highway Traffic Safety Administration (www.nhtsa.gov/) has been working to promote Vehicle to Vehicle (V2V) communication systems. "V2V communication enables vehicles to wirelessly exchange information about their speed, location, and heading. The technology behind V2V communication allows vehicles to broadcast and receive omni-directional messages (up to 10 times per second), creating a 360-degree 'awareness' of other vehicles in proximity. . . . V2V communication technology can increase the performance of vehicle safety systems and help save lives. There were an estimated 6.8 million police-reported crashes in 2019, resulting in 36,096 fatalities and an estimated 2.7 million people injured. Connected vehicle technologies will provide drivers with the tools they need to anticipate potential crashes and significantly reduce the number of lives lost each year."[5]

In addition to V2V communication, Vehicle to Infrastructure (V2I) communication is being designed, planned, and implemented. "V2I communication is the wireless exchange of data between vehicles and road infrastructure. Enabled by a system of hardware, software, and firmware, V2I communication is typically wireless and bi-directional: infrastructure components such as lane markings, road signs, and traffic

---

[4] Grace Kay, "A 1-mile stretch of road is being built in Detroit that can charge electric cars as they drive—if owners install a special receiver," *Business Insider*, Feb. 4, 2022, https://www.businessinsider.com/public-road-detroit-to-charge-electric-cars-as-they-drive-2022-2.

[5] "Vehicle-to-Vehicle Communication, Overview," *NHTSA*, cited Feb. 21, 2022, https://www.nhtsa.gov/technology-innovation/vehicle-vehicle-communication.

lights can wirelessly provide information to the vehicle, and vice versa. With so much data being captured, and shared, rich, timely information can be used to enable a wide range of safety, mobility, and environmental benefits."[6]

"To get the full benefit of connected and automated vehicles, you need the infrastructure outfitted. Infrastructure can carry and share information about crashes, traffic jams, sharp curves, and with recommended speeds. You can also dynamically change recommended speed based on weather or other conditions," remarked James Sayer of the University of Michigan Transportation Research Institute.[7]

With these new systems likely to be in place by 2025, our data generation on something as simple as a journey will quite simply be enormous.

8.3   *What's different in 2025?*

We just outlined what happens over two days, from the perspective of your data in a realistic scenario. Much of it sounded very similar to what happens today, and that is true, but there are a few significant differences. Among those changes, there are more data streams—the Vehicle 2 Vehicle (V2V) and Vehicle to Infrastructure (V2I) data streams are completely new. Many of the data streams are the same, such as texting, emailing, transactions, location, and video footage. Some of the data streams have gotten more granular and more common, such as the operational metrics from your electric vehicle as compared to a traditional gasoline powered automobile.

It may not be common knowledge that your electric vehicle comes with factory settings that share *all* the operational data generated by your car with the manufacturer. The manufacturer knows everything that happens in and around your car at all times. Be careful of those in-car cameras!

Your electric vehicle has more in common with your computers and their software than with your previous cars and trucks. The manufacturer of your electric vehicle sends and applies software updates to your car at regular intervals, and your car sends a continuous data stream back to the manufacturer about all operational aspects of your car and your use of your car.

There will be more monitoring and data at all levels. More speed monitoring along all types of roads—city, suburban, highway, rural. More video monitoring in cities. An increased number of satellites to capture, analyze, and understand weather, land use, building activity, troop movements, reforestation progress, sea levels, sea temperature, refugee movements, animal populations and migrations, whale populations and movements, and much more. There will be more and detailed information regarding the movements of individuals locally, nationally, and especially internationally.

Today we live in a world where EU citizens have more rights and abilities than other citizens, relating to data. In this section, we will assume that by 2025, many countries,

---

[6] "What is Vehicle-to-Infrastructure (V2I) Communication and why do we need it?," *3M*, cited Feb. 21, 2022, http://mng.bz/KlvK.

[7] Ibid.

states/provinces, and local jurisdictions will have the same or similar laws relating to our data. Perhaps that is wishful thinking, but we will go in that direction for now.

8.4 Data intermediaries (DIs)

Given all the data streams and data elements that we have discussed, it would be over-whelming for anyone to manage even one aspect of the relationship with the entirety of their data. Even if we limited our consideration to just one external party, asking an individual to manage their data in a comprehensive, cohesive, and proactive manner would be an impossible task, given the infrastructure that is in place today. In today's world, that is too much to ask of anyone, and that would be a very small part of the overall task of personally managing your data.

You, as an individual, will sign up to work with one or many data intermediaries (DIs). Those DIs will have relationships with all the companies, vendors, organizations, and governments you interact with.

8.4.1 Creation of DIs

National governments, through laws like the Data Act and Data Governance Act, will legally mandate that all firms, organizations, institutions, and governmental bodies that hold data about anybody will need to sign up with, and interact with, on an ongoing basis, all approved and certified DIs. You won't have to interact with all the vendors that you currently engage with and have engaged with over your lifetime to access, manage, and control your data and the data of your dependents. You will engage with one or more DIs.

8.4.2 A new regulatory environment for data

The market for DIs will grow substantially over the next few years. It will be large and significant, but governments will, in all likelihood, not let companies set up DI operations as a free-for-all. The market will be regulated, and a limited number of licenses will be granted. There will be competition, and multiple DIs will serve national and global markets. It will be like any other regulated industry. The data market, and industry, will operate under national and global supervision and regulation, just as the pharmaceutical, telecommunication, and finance markets and companies were established, have operated, and do operate.

There will not be thousands of DIs; perhaps there will be 40 to 60 on a global basis. The US may have approximately 10 to 15, the EU will have the same number. The UK will have 3 or 4. China will have 1, backed by the Chinese government, and it is more than likely that their market will be walled off from the rest of the world. Of course, they will want access to the data from the rest of the world without reciprocity. Russia will have a similar internal market as China, with similar rules and expectations. Japan, Korea, and other Asian countries will have 10 to 15 DIs, and Australia will have 3 or 4. The Middle East region will have 3 or 4. Africa could support a set of DIs, but we will see how the final distribution settles out in the coming years. Of course, there could be more or fewer DIs, but the scale and the global distribution outlined is roughly correct.

As we move forward, we will not describe the details of data storage or logical or physical data management environments. That would be too much technical detail (it is probably an entire book or multiple books unto itself). Those systems have yet to be physically designed. As we have discussed, the frameworks in the aforementioned laws are being drafted and passed, so we can predict what the conceptual design and operational framework will be.

8.4.3   *Managing your data in 2025*

As mandated by law, the DIs will have connections to all the vendors, governments, and organizations that hold and manage data about you and your interactions, transactions, texts, and any form of data you create, intentionally or not.

You will sign up with a DI, or DIs, through a standard account setup process. You will need to verify your identity, select your account settings and preferences, determine how to pay for your account, upload your credentials, picture, and other standard account initiation/verification information, and complete the process to establish your account(s).

Once your account is verified and active, then you will begin to connect your DI account to all the other accounts that are active today, those that were active, and organizations that have archival material about you that you want to have an active role in managing the storage, access, and use of. The majority of people will begin with their social media accounts. People will then move on to their offline accounts, such as telephone providers, internet providers, grocery stores, department stores, airline loyalty programs, credit scores/ratings, mortgage records, loan providers, extended warranty accounts, life insurance, disability insurance, utility providers, and municipal, state, and federal accounts. Remember, once the laws for your country, state/province, and locality are in place and can be enforced, you will have the right to access, manage, delete, and monetize every piece of data any organization possesses about you.

After the offline commercial accounts, people will start to connect to governmental accounts. In the US, those accounts include land records, tax records, Social Security, Medicaid, Medicare, veteran's affairs, scholarships, immigration records, passport, and citizenship records. There is no prescribed order for connecting your DI account with all the other accounts containing information stored about you and your activities. This order seems logical and natural to me, but you will be able to execute the process in any order that suits your objectives and ideals.

Once you have your DI account connected to all your accounts, or even to a subset of accounts, you can start to set up access rights—access rights for all organizations to access and use your information. Let's walk through an example rather than try to discuss this from a conceptual perspective.

There will be a variety of options for enabling and disabling access to your data. You may think and feel the way I do, in that there are certain companies I would never want to access any of my data. I will put a total block on all my data in relation to

Facebook, for example. I do not want Facebook to access any of my data, for any reason, at any price, at any time.

You may feel that a total block is not effective enough or does not send a strong enough message to the Facebook team. You may allow Facebook to access a subset of your data. When choosing the monetization settings, if the monetization settings available are between .001 of a cent and $1,000,000 per use, you could set the price to access this data element or these data elements at $1,000,000 for each access and use. Given that the price of accessing all data is zero today, $1,000,000 sends a strong and clear message to any company that you value your data.

8.5 Dimensions of data access

When you think about all your data, it is overwhelming to consider it as one entity. Instead, it is helpful to break the entire body of data about you and your activities down into consumable or manageable categories, such as browsing data, purchases, health care data, diagnostic records, travel data, location data, pictures, airline trips, grocery purchases, likes, electronics purchases, telephone calls, texts, posts, blogs, compliments, complaints, etc. The individual elements of your data are numerous and seemingly insurmountable to see as a unified whole. There are also, however, an endless number of ways to cluster, group, subset, segment, and organize your data into groups that make sense to you, the organizations, and other entities that want to access and leverage your data.

In the beginning, you will want to make it easy on yourself and simple for companies to understand whether they can include your data in their programs, projects, and efforts, and you will want to be clear about how much those companies must pay you for the use of your data. Do not be concerned about that aspect of the new world of data. Companies will bear the burden of understanding the cost of data and for paying you the rates you have set.

You can start with very broad categories, such as all purchases or transactions, or all the items you buy and have bought. That is a very extensive view of one section of your life and activity, and it is a very valuable collection of data. You could then break the purchase category down into purchases on Amazon, and for groceries, electronics, medical supplies, movies, entertainment, and sports. You could also create groups of purchases that are related to ski equipment, airfare, lodging, dining, and ski lessons. The examples of how to group and categorize your purchase data are limitless.

Historically, we know that the companies who make the most money from your data do so by selling groupings and categories of data that make advertisers feel like they have insight into, and are targeting and possibly reaching, the right audiences. If you want to make the most money from your data, you will want to package and group your data so that it is the most enticing to advertisers. Take a look at figure 8.1. Those who have our data today are making billions from it, and they will pay to continue to be able to do so.[8]

---

[8] LinkedIn post from Kimberly Wright, cited February 20, 2022.

Figure 8.1   Google Data (Source: LinkedIn post from Kimberly Wright, cited February 20, 2022.)

It is not often that we experience the creation of an entirely new aspect of our global economic system. We will see this unfold in front of us over the next few years.

8.6   *What DIs will do for you*

DIs will provide the tools, technologies, connections, and engaging user interfaces required for you to group, segment, and present your data in the most compelling manner, if you are inclined to organize your data yourself. I anticipate that most people will not want to try to organize their data into groups and categories in ways that will map to, and maximize, their goals and values. It will be challenging enough for most people to map their data-related objectives to their own values, goals, and ideals.

I expect that most readers of this book will know what their values, goals, and ideals are, and how those guideposts in life relate and map to their data objectives. For most of the population, it will take a bit of thought and introspection to arrive at that level of awareness. My prediction is that DIs will provide services that will make it very easy for everyone to align their data objectives with their overarching goals, values, and ideals.

8.6.1 *Setting revenue maximization as your primary objective*

DIs will have access to data from millions of people, and they will constantly analyze the data to glean insights into sources of demand, price points, access frequency, industries, and companies. If the laws around the world follow the EU model, DIs will be prohibited from selling data. They will only be allowed to access, protect, and organize data. Of course, DIs will sell other services, but they will be barred from direct data sales. Since they can't sell data, they will be committed to the goal of making your data accessible, usable, valuable, and easy to leverage both for you and for the companies that want to use our data in their commercial efforts.

If your primary objective is maximizing revenue to you, the DIs will have analyzed the national, international, regional/provincial, and local market for companies that want to purchase and use data similar to yours. DIs will be able to tell you which groups and categories of data are in demand and the market price that is being paid for that data. They will be able to outline the demand and price for mass market data, specialty data, low volume data, data for targeting consumer goods, data relevant to enterprise class companies, sporting and recreational audiences, industrial companies, not for profits, special interest groups, community groups, self help and support groups, faith-based organizations, veterans, and many more. DIs will offer many services, among them a service that you will pay for that will organize your data elements and sources into a cohesive whole that is attractive to data buyers of all the categories I just listed.

My prediction is that the data market will operate much like all open markets. The most relevant comparison that comes to mind is the commodities markets—gold, corn, wheat, rye, coal, etc. The data markets will evolve in sophistication over time. In the beginning, DIs will be the middlemen, but over time they will become brokers, dealers and specialists that serve the producers of data, us, and the buyers of data.

I expect that DIs will compete to have the broadest number of connections with as many companies as possible. This will give them access to the most data. In turn, the DIs will be able to offer the most value-added services to data producers and data consumers.

8.6.2 *Many objectives*

When you sign into your DI account, you will select your primary objective, such as revenue maximization. The DI software will know what data you have to offer and the market and prices being offered for that data as individual elements in various markets around the world. Also, the DI's software will also know the millions, if not billions or trillions of combinations that your data can be combined into and the resulting revenue that you will be paid. Furthermore, the DIs will know what other data your data should be combined with to make it the most valuable as a larger collection of data.

Integrating your data into larger groups can be done within your data sets. Combining your purchase data category with your browsing data category would be a common integration. Integrating your in-store grocery purchases with your online grocery purchases would provide a complete wallet share of your grocery spending. Your data could be integrated with data of other people who have similar or dissimilar habits, lifestyles, or economic status and could be done in many ways using the following dimensions: age, gender, location, time, season, affinities, price points, life stage, family size. Those and many other descriptors can be used to create new groupings of data that are of keen interest to companies.

Integrating and grouping data is a simple process of data management. Any true data company can do this. DIs are and will be the next generation of data companies. Their *raison d' etre* is to manage data and make data easy to access, describe, manage, price, group, and sell.

I envision you will be able to set a combination of parameters and objectives that enable the DIs to access and understand all your objectives—not just your primary objectives, but all the objectives you set. You won't set these objectives all at one time and leave them. As your needs, wants, and life stage changes, so will your objectives for your data. Over time you will add, delete, and modify your objectives to meet your needs. You may have thousands of objectives. One of the roles of the DIs is to help you manage and maintain your objectives so that your data serves you and your needs.

The more sophisticated DIs will have simulation software that will run on a continuous basis and will provide all data creators with updates and suggestions on how to update and modify the conditions and prices at which you offer your data. The top-level DIs will be scanning the markets, seeing opportunities, and alerting you to new combinations and integrations of data that you can be part of. All you will have to do is to accept or deny the offers to join these integrations and combinations.

The most sophisticated DIs will have optimization software that will aggregate the billions of offers, prices, and data integrations to optimize your stated objectives, and they may even offer you suggestions on new data-related objectives that align with the aggregate of your stated objectives.

You will set your objective, such as for revenue maximization, the DI's software will have a catalog of all your data and will know the market and prices for your data. The DI's software will make recommendations to add, change, or extend your objectives or to set them for the first time, and all you will have to do is click Accept.

This is a case where artificial intelligence (AI) will be key to staying up to date with all the changes in your objectives, data markets, prices offered, and data legislation. AI will make the data markets more dynamic, in general, and user friendly for the billions of data producers.

8.6.3   *Setting multiple objectives*

As we have been discussing, you will be managing your data through your relationship with a DI. You will have several objectives and goals that help you align the deployment and use of your data with your values. If you are concerned about global warming, you can make your data or any subset of your data available to firms that support improving the global climate on very advantageous terms. You might even be able to pay those firms for using your data. On the reverse side, you can ban firms that you feel are not supporting the improvement of the global climate from using your data, or charge an exorbitant amount of money for them to access and use your data. You will be able to set objectives for each element of data, any grouping of data, and any integration of your data with any other set of data from individuals around the world.

Let's say that you have developed a rare disease—a disease that only afflicts 10,000 people in the world. You would probably want to integrate your medical records, diagnostic history, prescription records, genetic sequence, and maybe more data with the other people impacted by the same disease. This overall group can offer greater utility and benefit to researchers and drug developers than each of you could alone. The unified data set would enable researchers to understand the totality of the population affected and the detailed characteristics of the disease. If everyone in the group contributed their genetic sequencing, the researchers could work with an entire census of the population, and the insights to be gained could be very useful.

Let's take this example one step further. A hypothetical pharmaceutical company is working on a therapy to lessen the effects of the disease to improve the quality of life of the patients. Another company is working on a gene therapy that could possibly cure the disease. Which do you support with your data? You could support both, of course, but do you have a preference? If you do, you can make that clear through your choices in your data objectives.

Let's extend this example just one more step. What if your data contributions could pay for the conventional therapy for the remainder of your life but only for a small portion of the cure? Would that change how you would set your data objectives? Something to think about ….

You could be very creative and inventive in how you categorize, subset, segment, price, and limit access to all or parts of your data. Or you could be very restrictive in how you categorize, subset, segment, and limit access to all or parts of your data. You could set up restrictions so that no company in Russia could use your data, or perhaps no company outside the region where a transaction took place could access the data. Perhaps you don't agree with oil companies, and you don't want any companies involved in the exploration, discovery, drilling, refining, distributing, or selling of oil to even know that your data exists. No problem—with the click of a button, you can block all oil companies from having access to your data.

Or you can be completely open, and you can set access rights on all your purchase or transaction data so that all companies can access and use your transactional data in their targeting, marketing, analytics, and other use cases without limitations and without fees. I am not sure why you would do that, but you could.

Now, let's talk about data monetization in more detail.

8.7   *Dimensions of data monetization*

When you're thinking about monetizing your data, keep your mind as open as possible. Why? Data is a valuable commodity. Remember in chapter 6 when we talked about the $3 trillion dollars in market value that will be generated through the data economy? A substantial portion of that money will be paid to people who generate data—that is a dramatic change in monetary flows.

Data has several characteristics that make it not only valuable, but unique. "Data has unique characteristics that make it potentially more valuable than oil: it can be reused over and over, it can be used multiple ways simultaneously, and whoever uses data generates more data."[9] Data is very different from the traditional commodities that we are accustomed to: it doesn't wear out, it gets more valuable as you accumulate it, it can be integrated in unlimited ways, it is easily transported around the world with almost no cost, and it has unique scarcity/abundance properties. For all these reasons, the view we need to take on monetizing data is different than if we were thinking about gold, oil, cash, or diamonds.

Doug Laney has written the definitive book on understanding the underlying economics of data: *Infonomics.*[10] We will not be exploring those topics and considerations here, so pick up Laney's book if you want to take a deep dive into the economic underpinnings of data.

What we are going to discuss in this section is the practical matter of, and the considerations leading to, you making money, or driving value with your data. The first topic people ask me about is getting paid for the use of your data. That is of great interest, and it is a good start, but that is only the most obvious payment pathway.

As we have discussed, DIs have been and will be created to be your interface to your data. Their business will be to help you understand how to realize your objectives and goals when it comes to your data, including getting paid on a regular basis. You will have an account at your primary DI, and through that account you will be connected to all DIs operating around the world. We have discussed that you will be able to set your price, access rights, total blocks, and many other settings in relation to your data. You will also be able to take advantage of the intelligence that your primary DI and all the other DIs have created about data, markets, prices, and demand.

Beyond data consumers accessing and paying for the use of your data, you can pay organizations to use your data. Let's say that you believe strongly in supporting efforts to deliver clean drinking water to all parts of the world. There are many charity organizations focused on this cause. You research and find one that you like, care for, and want to be aligned with. You can set a data objective that each time the charity accesses and uses your data, for any purpose, it triggers an automatic payment from your account at the DI for a predetermined amount that you set. The payment could be a penny, or a dollar, or the entire amount in your DI account. You decide. It is real money.

---

[9] Doug Laney, Twitter post, cited Mar 1, 2022, http://mng.bz/91gl.
[10] Doug Laney, *Infonomics: How to Monetize, Manage, and Measure Information as an Asset for Competitive Advantage* (Routledge, 2017).

The DI accounts can be transferable to children or others you want to support for whatever reason, including educational and medical institutions. You could set up your DI account to accumulate payments and interest until the date arrives when you want to begin that support. As qualified expenses present themselves, you can trigger a payment to them, to their parents, or to the appropriate organization to pay their expenses.

These are not credits—this is not funny money. This is real legal tender, and you can spend it any way you want. Spend it on your rent, your mortgage, car repairs, donate it to charity, go out to dinner. You name it, you can spend your data dividend on it.

8.7.1 How much money will your data dividend be?

How much the data dividend will be is pure speculation. No one really knows. Not all data will be valued in the same way.

The history of what companies like Amazon, Facebook, Netflix, and others have charged for access to and the use of data will in all likelihood set a benchmark for where pricing decisions and discussion will begin. In general, markets change gradually, and the data market will be no different.

Your economic status will also play a part in the value placed on your data in the open market. People who buy and spend more and in greater amounts will probably be paid more than those who buy and spend less in lesser amounts—that is from a purely commercial perspective.

Your health status will play a part in valuing your data. People who have rare diseases or highly unusual blood types or disorders may be able to demand a premium price for their diagnostic and prescription history, medical records, and genetic material and sequencing.

Where you live will play a part in data pricing, as will numerous other factors, such as your life stage, marital status, income, location, home ownership, debt level, and many more.

We discussed the music royalty systems in chapter 4. Bands like Led Zeppelin and ZZ Top make more from royalties than do The Thompson Twins or Thomas Dolby. The data market will operate on a similar principle. There will be data that is more popular and therefore more valuable than other data, and the more valuable data will likely be accessed more often and used more frequently by a wider range of companies.

In an article on Forbes.com, Sean Herman undertook the effort to calculate what a data dividend would look like if it were based on company profits. He used Facebook as his example and calculated the following:

> *What if Facebook was an equitable business partner that shared half of its profit with those of us who actually provide the data that makes its business model run? Using my math (which is, again, open to debate), the average Facebook user would earn $10.77 per quarter. But, what if you are a more active user than average? Twice as active? Five times as active? Out of curiosity, I broke the numbers down below.*

- *Half as active: $5.38*
- *Twice as active: $21.53*
- *Five times as active: $53.83*
- *Ten times as active: $107.67[11]*

Using Herman's methodology, if you were on 15 applications and platforms and you were an average user, your data dividend would be $646.20 each year.

I appreciate Sean Herman's efforts, and I think that he did a great job of calculating a baseline, but I believe that this methodology undervalues the data dividend by at least half for an average active user. I am not sure about you, but I would be happy with an additional $600 to $1,300 dollars per year for doing nothing more than I do today.

Herman used company profits as the metric from which he calculated his version of a data dividend. Company profit is completely under the control of every company and can be manipulated in many ways. My view is that the data dividend should be a product of an open market and subject to the factors of supply and demand. I could be way off in my estimate of the annual data dividend, but in my view there could be people who make over $20,000 to $50,000 or more each year from licensing their personal data.

8.7.2   *Data ownership and licensing*

Take note of the word *licensing*. You will not sell your data to companies; you will license it. You will retain ownership of the data, and you will provide a limited use license to your data. Do not be concerned about needing to develop a licensing agreement; this is another service that your DI will provide. The DIs will have standard licensing agreements that you can use.

This is a common practice for software and technology. You use software from Microsoft and other companies, but you don't own it—you have a limited use license to use the software. You can't change it or improve the software; you can only use it as the software vendor has determined in the licensing agreement that you "signed" but probably did not read.

You will license your data to others for specific uses. Let's walk through a quick example. Let's say that Unilever licenses your data, and data from millions of people like you, to analyze, understand, and formulate products, messages, and marketing campaigns related to toothpaste. That is fine. You want better toothpaste, and you have no issue with Unilever, and the rate they are paying is above the market rate for your personal hygiene products purchasing, use, and opinions. Now, if Unilever wants to do the same thing for deodorant, they must license your data again and pay you again, because the first licensing agreement limited the use to one product category, toothpaste. You can limit the use of your data in any way that makes sense to you and that the companies are willing to agree to. As I always say about contracts and licensing agreements, if you can think it or say it, you can write it into an agreement. The only limit is your imagination.

---

[11]Sean Herman, "Should Tech Companies Be Paying Us For Our Data?" *Forbes*, Oct. 30, 2020, https://www.forbes.com/sites/forbestechcouncil/2020/10/30/should-tech-companies-be-paying-us-for-our-data/.

8.7.3 Beyond the cash, what is the value to you?

Let's think about this from a perspective of overall value to you. Think of any category of spending—hotels, groceries, airfare, vacation travel, energy, electronics, charitable giving. Businesses generally want to either acquire new customers or entice existing customers to spend more with them rather than the alternatives. In this new world, you will be able to share with and illustrate to any business your entire spending in the relevant category.

Perhaps you have seen surveys like this one: you are asked how many airline trips you have taken in the last year for business and for leisure. You are asked which carriers you traveled on. The airline is attempting to determine your total spending on airfare and their share of your wallet or spending in the previous year. They assume that most people will be reasonably accurate in reporting their spending, but, as surveys go, you can never be assured that the data reported is completely accurate. As a data and analytics professional, I am always skeptical of self-reported data; I prefer transactions or verified data.

In the new data world, you can designate that all your spending on airfare is available to one carrier, say American Airlines; or all carriers in the US; or all carriers in the US, Canada, and Western Europe; or all carriers in Asia and Australia but not Thai Airlines (for some personal reason); or any combination of carriers that you include or exclude for reasons that make sense to you; or all carriers without limitation. The carriers will pay you to access your spending on airline travel, and then they will determine how to market to you and what offers and discounts they want to provide to you to entice you to spend your airline funds with them. This is a much more transparent, data driven way to determine the level of relationship the carrier wants with you and you with them.

What value is that? I'd say it is valuable from the view of convenience, quality of service, and total price. You are putting the burden of convincing you which is the best airline and the best economic value on the carriers. They are paying you, which is nice, to compete for your business, which is even better. Why spend all that time trying to find the best deal when the airlines can compete to give you the best deal. I am not sure about you, but my time is very valuable. I'd rather have companies working to make me happy rather than me trying to dig up the best deal possible. Data has the potential to flip the script on many existing relationships. I want companies working to make me happy; how about you?

8.8 So what do we do today?

Today you can't control your data in an easy and simple manner. Even the citizens of the EU and UK, who have many more rights and protections than the rest of us, still have a challenging time instructing companies to manage and delete data in accordance with their wishes. What can you do today?

First, don't do business with companies that you know are hurting you, your family, your communities, your country, and the world. If you are involved with such a company, stop using their service, delete all your data, and tell all your friends to stop using the platform.

Second, sign up for every "do not mail" list that you can. It doesn't take long, and it really works. Most of our discussions have been about online data, and that is the most important category, but companies still mail a significant amount of material. The lists and data being held by those companies are significant, and those companies are the most aggressive resellers of your data. Getting off and out of their lists should be a priority for everyone.

After we signed up on all the do-not-mail lists that we could find, we went from getting 8 to 12 pieces of physical mail each day to perhaps 1 or 2 pieces a week. I took the additional step of calling every company that was sending us physical mail, and those sending mail to the people who lived at our address previously but have been dead for over 15 years. I asked each company to put each name on their do-not-mail lists. This reduces the data about you that is active and can be sold, and it helps the planet by reducing the printed material and the time, energy, and cost of mailing all this useless material.

Third, sign up for every "do not call" list that you can. The results are the same as above, but just on your mobile device. I block every spam call that makes it to my mobile device. This is a little more time consuming, but it does cut down on the number of calls that you will receive. The calls are annoying, but if you block them, the calling companies will remove your number from the calling lists, thereby reducing the data that is active and circulating about you.

Fourth, be careful when doing anything online. It sounds like overkill, but when you are about to apply for a job, scroll down. If you look, I bet there is a checkbox checked that says something like, "Follow this company" or "Sign up for our mailing list." It seems small, but every one of these lists that you avoid reduces the data about you floating around for someone to buy and to aggregate into a new list to send messages to. This is not just related to job applications; it really applies to anything. Buying clothes—opt out of following the company. Buying camping supplies—ensure that you are opted out. It makes a big difference. No surprise here. I do this on every transaction.

8.9   Final thoughts

Clearly, I feel a sense of passion and commitment to the topic of data. I have spent the past 37 years of my life—my entire career—immersed in data. Data is very important to all of us; many of us just don't know it yet. I wanted you to know that the world of data that we live in today did not come about by happenstance; it was designed and built on purpose. It was useful and valuable 100 years ago, but now it must go.

Over the past century, entrepreneurs, business executives, and businesses have taken advantage of this data landscape for their own advantage, and good for them in many cases. They have delivered valuable services and insights for all of us across every industry. Now we find ourselves in a new world, an emerging world, where data is different. The data of the past is not the data of today, and it's certainly not the data of the future.

People said that internet connectivity is the same no matter what, but that premise has been proven to be patently false. Dial-up internet access in the hands of a few enthusiasts is not the same as ubiquitous, high-speed broadband to every person everywhere. The opportunities afforded by the latter are immense. The former was great, but it was really the first phase of something much greater, much more valuable, and much more interesting for all of us.

Just as high-speed broadband to every mobile device, household, and office changed the way everyone worked, accessed content, created content, became consistently connected and universally engaged, the new world of data will change everything that we know and do.

I am keen for everyone to know about the flawed data ownership model that has persisted since the beginning of the modern data industry. Companies knew and still know that they are making money from a commodity that they do not own. We own it, and they know it. This will change, this must change, this is changing.

In the past, data ownership didn't matter much to the general population, given that the economics of monetizing an individual's data was not very compelling, but it is compelling for some today and it will be compelling for all very soon. I wanted everyone to know about all the global legislative changes that are underway and those that will be coming. Knowing the history of data, your current relationship with data, and how that needs to change through the law and legislation is key to being aware and in a place where you can benefit from the new world of data.

As we all now know, we will explicitly own our own data. Our rights will be ensconced in law. We will be able to manage our data like we do any other asset. We will monetize and control our data to our benefit.

I feel that it is important for you to know and understand how trust plays an important role in your relationship with your data and the organizations that want to use your data. As with all relationships, we need to have a baseline of trust. If trust is not there, the relationship will not grow and prosper.

I wanted you to know and to understand your right to privacy and why that is important not only legally, but cognitively and psychologically. We have a vague understanding of our right to privacy. Most of this has been driven by legislative action and reaction by companies, mostly so they can avoid making real and meaningful changes, but we as humans need privacy, and it is good to have a deeper understanding of this basic need and our rights. I know that we only touched the surface, but it is good for all of us to know a bit more about this core area of our psychology.

I feel that it is imperative for the people who read this book to be aware of the massive latent amount of economic value that will be created through the new world of data and that the economic value will be more evenly distributed if we, as a group of empowered people, act to make it so. This is not some pie-in-the-sky, altruistic endeavor—we all can benefit. All the world can benefit from ensuring that the new world of data delivers economic value to the true owners of data, us.

There is a sea change that is slowly moving its way through societies, national and international governing bodies, state and provincial governments, and local communities. It is going to be a fraught process. Companies that are making billions of dollars from our data will fight with all their energy to stop, slow, or derail this movement, but they will fail.

The Future of Data is ours and for us to benefit from. Let's go take it!

Summary

- Data as a commodity has unique characteristics, and we need to understand how data is different from gold, oil, or other commodities so that we can use data to its fullest.
- Given the unique characteristics of data, we can aggregate, group, integrate, and use data in many ways. This affords us the opportunity to set many interlocking or separate objectives for our data use and data monetization.
- DIs are a new type of company that will be mandated by law and governed in ways that make them useful and valuable to everyone in managing their data.
- The sophistication of managing your data will grow in time, and you will manage your data to match the objectives that support your life, values, and needs.
- You can start to manage your data today.

index

RELATED MANNING TITLES

Data Privacy
by Nishant Bhajaria

ISBN 9781617298998
384 pages, $49.99
January 2022

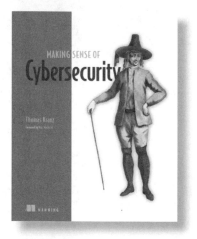

Making Sense of Cybersecurity
by Thomas Kranz
Foreword by Naz Markuta

ISBN 9781617298004
288 pages, $49.99
October 2022

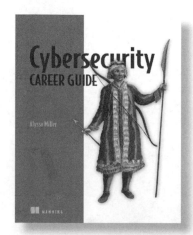

Cybersecurity Career Guide
by Alyssa Miller

ISBN 9781617298202
200 pages, $49.99
May 2022

For ordering information, go to www.manning.com